Indianisation of English
Analysis of Linguistic Features in Selected Post-1980 Indian English Fiction

The Author

Dr. Sumana Bandyopadhyay, obtained her first class Master's Degree in Linguistics from Calcutta University in 2000, and her Ph.D. Degree from the Indian Institute of Technology, Kanpur in 2008. She was Project Associate in R and D, Ministry of Science and Technology, Government of India, Speech Recognition Project at IIT, Kanpur. Dr. Bandyopadhyay has three papers to her credit and has lectured at various professional bodies. She is currently working on Cognitive Linguistics. She is a life member of the Linguistic Society of India and the Dravidian Linguistics Association.

Indianisation of English

Analysis of Linguistic Features in Selected Post-1980 Indian English Fiction

Sumana Bandyopadhyay

CONCEPT PUBLISHING COMPANY PVT. LTD.
NEW DELHI-110059

ISBN-13-978-81-8069-703-6

First Published 2010

Published and Printed by

Concept Publishing Company Pvt. Ltd.
Regd. Office:
A/15-16, Commercial Block, Mohan Garden
New Delhi-110059 (India)
Phones : 25351460, 25351794, *Fax* : 091-11-25357109
Email : publishing@conceptpub.com
Website: www.conceptpub.com

Editorial Office:
H-13, Bali Nagar, New Delhi-110 015, India

Cataloging in Publication Data--*Courtesy:* D.K. Agencies (P) Ltd. <docinfo@dkagencies.com>

Bandyopadhyay, Sumana.
Indianisation of English : analysis of linguistic features in selected post-1980 Indian English fiction / Sumana Bandyopadhyay.
p. cm.
Includes bibliographical references (p.).
Includes index.
ISBN 13: 9788180697036

1. Indic fiction (English)--20th century--History and criticism. 2. English literature-Indic influences. 3. English language--Variation--India. I. Title.

DDC 823.9109954 22

Dedication

The book is dedicated

to

My Parents

Foreword

Dr. Christopher Rollason

The present study, by Sumana Bandyopadhyay of the Indian Institute of Technology, Kanpur, is entitled *Indianisation of English: Analysis of Linguistic Features in Selected Post-1980 Indian English Fiction*, and is offered as an overview of a number of key linguistic aspects of the English language as used in a particular register — the literary one — in the second-language setting and multilingual context of contemporary India.

India is a land where multilingualism is a way of life,[1] as its inhabitants are reminded every time they handle a national banknote featuring 17 languages.[2] The total number of mother tongues spoken in India is, according to the census for which the most recent data exist, that of 1991, 1576.[3] 23 languages currently have constitutional status, and 22 of those are listed in the Eighth Schedule to the Constitution of India. In the wake of Independence, these initially numbered 14; this list has been extended over the years by a number of constitutional amendments, of which the most recent, the Ninety-Second of 2004, added another four languages.[4] The 22 are, in alphabetical order: Assamese, Bengali, Bodo, Dogri, Gujarati, Hindi, Kannada, Kashmiri, Konkani, Maithili, Malayalam, Manipuri, Marathi, Nepali, Oriya, Punjabi, Sanskrit, Santhali, Sindhi, Tamil, Telugu and Urdu.[5] Of these, four belong to the Dravidian group (Kannada, Malayalam, Tamil and Telugu), two are Tibeto-Burmese (Bodo and Manipuri), one is Austro-Asiatic (Santhali), and the remaining 15 are Indo-Aryan (a subset of Indo-European). To these 22 should be added a 23rd, namely English (also Indo-European), which has the special constitutional status of *associate official language* alongside Hindi. The multilingual situation is further complicated by the fact that no single language — and that includes Hindi — is spoken as a first language by a majority of India's population. Multilingualism is an all but banal component of daily life throughout India, be it in homes, shops, markets, transport, banks, businesses, etc. Many individuals are trilingual or quadrilingual, and code-switching and code-mixing are everyday occurrences.

Article 343 of the Constitution of India as originally framed states in its first paragraph: "The official language of the Union shall be Hindi," but goes on to add in the second paragraph: "For a period of fifteen years from the commencement of this Constitution, the English language shall continue to be used for all the official purposes of the Union for which it was being used immediately before such commencement," and, in the third paragraph: "Parliament may by law provide for the use, after the said period of fifteen years, of ... the English language ... for such purposes as are specified in the law."[6] In other words, the constitutional text opened the possibility of dropping English after fifteen years, while simultaneously maintaining the alternative option of continuing to use it indefinitely. In fact, it was decided in the Official Languages Act of 1963 to retain English with its existing status, and today, more than forty years on, that remains the option which has prevailed[7].

The real number of English users in today's India is something of a vexed question. Those who use English are a quantitatively large, proportionately small and disproportionately influential minority of Indians. Estimates of the percentage of the population who use English (depending obviously on what that means, in terms of sociolinguistic context, first, second or third language, active versus passive, spoken versus written, degree of competence, etc.) vary enormously, ranging from 2-4 per cent to 10-20 per cent. Traditionally estimates have been on the lower side, but there is now a tendency to up the figures. The influential British linguist David Graddol states that "India contains a significant proportion of the world's speakers of English as a second language, but estimating the number of L2 speakers of English there is difficult," and, while noting a consensus among linguists in the past "that around 4 per cent of the Indian population speaks English as a second language," contends that "there is evidence ... that the number ... is higher than this," even positing a figure approaching 20 per cent for those "confident of speaking" the language.[8] Another expert, Tom McArthur, suggests that "there may well be *c.* 100-200 million people using the language regularly" and that "an expanding middle class increasingly uses it, and seeks it for their children, and for that group 10 per cent of the population is not an unlikely base figure."[9] The 1991 census gives a mere 178, 598 (or 0.021 per cent of the population) declaring English as their *first* language, but for the proportion of the total population with English as their *second* or *third* language, offers 8 per cent plus 3.1 per cent respectively.[10] This would amount to some 90 million English speakers, i.e. considerably more than the total in the UK.

The accumulated presence of English in the education system is such that some educated Indians not only write by preference in English but admit that they speak and even think in English first, keeping other languages mostly for communication with those like servants or taxi-drivers. Annika Hohenthal, a Finnish linguist, comments: "English is virtually the first language for many educated Indians, and for many who speak more than one language, English is the second one." Nonetheless, Hohenthal further observes that, unlike in some parts of the world, "English has not driven out any of the indigenous languages, existing, rather, alongside them."[11] It is interesting to note that another language scholar, B. Mallikarjun — writing in the same journal as Hohenthal — makes similar claims for Hindi: "The Indian social and political set-up has allowed Hindi to create space for its growth without forcing other languages from their own space ... It has become an additional language and not a substitute language."[12] At all events, when it comes to international relations, it is English that prevails. English is employed for communication with the rest of the subcontinent (Pakistan, Bangladesh, Nepal and Sri Lanka all continue to use English) and with the wider world — notably, of course, today in India's burgeoning "new sectors" such as software development, BPO (business process outsourcing), biotechnology, pharmaceuticals, etc.

India is, besides, one of the world's most prolific countries in book production, with vast numbers of titles appearing every year, in every major Indian language and in English. More titles are published in English than in any other language: official figures for 1995-96 gave a total of 14,883 books published in India, of which 5,907 (39.68 per cent) were in English.[13] India is generally said to be the world's third largest producer of books in English, after the US and the UK. The capital's Darya Ganj quarter boasts a whole collection of streets playing host to the offices and warehouses of, in many cases, English-language publishers. A typical English-language bookshop will, while not neglecting the Dan Browns and J.K. Rowlings and offering a range of British and American books on import, stock mostly fiction and non-fiction published in India, written directly in English, by Indians and for Indians. Most of this material has traditionally not been exported outside the subcontinent, though of course today Indian titles may be purchased on-line from anywhere in the world. Apart from literature proper, more than worthy of attention is the very large number of endogenous non-fiction titles, academic or otherwise, in English. Indeed, such is the critical mass of academic titles alone in English that the serried ranks of those books constitute in themselves a clear argument for India needing to retain English: the labour of translating them all into Indian languages would be more than herculean. The press, for its part, flourishes in the whole range of languages: 1997 figures affirmed the existence of 5,200 newspapers in India, with a total circulation, all languages combined, of 105 million.[14] The leading English-language title, *The Times of India*, which dates from 1838 and has editions published from ten Indian cities, at that time proclaimed a circulation of 1.4 million,[15] and has since rebranded itself as the world's biggest-circulation English-language substantive newspaper.[16] The big English-language national dailies, with their regional editions, have the advantage of being read all over the country, albeit figures released in 1999 nonetheless revealed that in India as a whole "all the top ten dailies ... were Indian-language newspapers," with the largest circulation (9.45 million) accruing to the Tamil daily *Dina Thanthi*. However, the English-language press, which also includes glossy political weeklies such as *India Today* and less cerebral publications like *Stardust*, is still considered "the most resource-endowed sector within the Indian press,"[17] and foreign visitors may be struck by the way good hotels may offer up to a dozen newspapers for perusal, all in English but all Indian.

* * * * * * * *

Since English is, willy-nilly, India's main linguistic conduit to a wider world that increasingly needs India, it will now be of interest, in the context of the present volume, to take a closer look at some aspects of the nature and functions of Indian English, and, subsequently, at the literary phenomenon known as Indian Writing in English (or IWE).

English has been spoken in the subcontinent since the first wave of British traders and adventurers arrived around 1600, but today's boom in English-language services for the world market may be seen as an unintended effect of Thomas Babington Macaulay's celebrated project of teaching English to Indians, which laid the bases for India's British-style education system, along lines still extant today. In a more than famous passage of his "Minute on Indian Education" of 1835 — by now all but quoted to death — Macaulay, in his capacity as member of the Supreme Council of India and President of the Committee of Public Instruction, set out a blueprint for the organised teaching of English to India's native elite, stating the goal of creating "a class who may be interpreters between us and the millions whom we govern; a class of persons, Indian in blood and colour, but English in taste, in opinions, in morals, and in intellect." That passage is traditionally quoted as epitomising an oppressive linguistic colonialism. It is, however, less often observed that Macaulay and his fellow "Anglicists" were promoting English not so much against Indian vernacular languages as, rather, against the rival "Orientalist" claims of Sanskrit, Persian and Arabic. Today, Chandra Bhan Prasad, an iconoclastic newspaper columnist of Dalit origin and tireless advocate for the rights of his community,[18] has suggested an alternative, and more contextual reading:

> Was Macaulay writing a secret book to "enslave" Indians

> mentally, and perpetuate ignorance among natives? ... While Orientalists sang the praises of India's past, Anglicists were confronting the backwardness and obscurantism of Hindu and Muslim cultures, their ethos, their rituals. They thought that the true god of Indians could only be modernity — the sciences, mechanics, European philosophy ... The full text of Macaulay's Minute shows him passionately arguing for modern scientific education for native Indians, and thus exposing the backwardness of indigenous systems.[19]

Prasad also reminds the modern reader that Macaulay goes on to suggest that the use of English will have a trickle-down, modernising effect on the vernacular languages (which the nineteenth century writer misleadingly terms "dialects"): "To that class we may leave it to refine the vernacular dialects of the country, to enrich those dialects with terms of science borrowed from the Western nomenclature, and to render them by degrees fit vehicles for conveying knowledge to the great mass of the population." Macaulay, further and interestingly, states that many educated Indians already have a highly sophisticated grasp of English, extending to the technical and literary registers and permitting the understanding of "even the more delicate graces of our most idiomatic writers": "There are (...) natives who are quite competent to discuss political or scientific questions with fluency and precision in the English language (...) Indeed it is unusual to find, even in the literary circles of the [European] continent, any foreigner who can express himself in English with so much facility and correctness as we find in many Hindoos."[20]

Today, over half a century after the departure of the British, India uses English not less but more than it did under the Raj—but *voluntarily*, and *no longer precisely the same English*. The former colonial language has over time been appropriated and adapted to specifically Indian ends of nationwide diffusion and communication, with a free admixture of terms from autochthonous tongues: the interaction between English and Indian languages ran (and runs) parallel with other and multiple forms of interaction among the Indian languages themselves.

If we move on from Macaulay, we find that in an essay of 1854, "The Anglo-Saxon and the Hindu," the Bengali writer Michael Madhusudan Dutt made the remarkably anglophile statement: "I love the language of the Anglo-Saxon ... My imagination visions forth before me the language of the Anglo-Saxon in all its radiant beauty; and I feel silenced and abashed."[21] By contrast, Dutt's fellow Bengali, Bankim Chandra Chatterjee, in "A Popular Literature for Bengal," a paper read — albeit in English — to the Bengal Social Science Association in 1870, declared:

> ... a single great idea, communicated to the people of Bengal in their own language, circulated among them in the language that alone touches their hearts, vivifying and permeating the conceptions of all ranks, will work out grander results than all that our English speeches and preachings will ever be able to achieve.[22]

The debate continues to rage, notably in literary circles and fuelled by both creative writers and critics, as to whether English is by now an "Indian language" or not. Raja Rao famously argued in 1938, in the preface to his celebrated novel *Kanthapura*, for using *English, but an English adapted to Indian conditions*:

> English is not really an alien language to us. It is the language of our intellectual make-up — like Sanskrit or Persian was before — but not of our emotional make-up. We are all instinctively bilingual, many of us in our own language and in English. We cannot write like the English. We should not. We can only write as Indians (...) Our method of expression ... will some day prove to be as distinctive and colourful as the Irish or the American.[23]

A.K. Ramanujan, in an essay of 1989 entitled "Is There An Indian Way of Thinking?", argued, somewhat provocatively, that an analogy exists between English and Sanskrit:

> When English is borrowed into (or imposed on) Indian contexts, it fits into the Sanskrit slot; it acquires many of the characteristics of Sanskrit, the older native father tongue, its pan-Indian elite character — as a medium of laws, science and administration, and its formulaic patterns; it becomes part of Indian multiple diglossia.[24]

Strong doubts are, though, still expressed today over the validity of Indians writing in English, even by writers who have made their names through the medium of that language. We may note the terse remark of a character in *The Dark Holds No Terrors*, a novel of 1980 by Shashi Deshpande: "After all, it isn't our language."[25] The dilemma is articulated by Vikram Chandra, in a passage (paradoxically written in eloquent English) in his novel of 1995, *Red Earth and Pouring Rain*:

> How in English can one say roses, doomed love, chaste passion, my father my mother, their love which never spoke, pride, honour, what a man can live for and what a woman should die for, how in English can one say the cows' slow distant tinkle at sunset, the green weight of the trees after monsoon, dust of winnowing and women's songs, elegant shadow of a minar creeping across white marble, the patient goodness of people met at wayside, the enfolding trust of aunts and uncles and cousins, winter bonfires and fresh chapattis, in English all this, the true shape and contour of a nation's heart, all this is left unsaid and unspeakable and invisible.[26]

Conversely, however, Salman Rushdie, in an essay of 1983, stressed the role of English in India as a bridging language between communities and regions, arguing:

> ... the children of independent India seem not to think of English as being irredeemably tainted by its colonial provenance. They use it as an Indian language, as one of the tools they have to hand ... In South India ... the

> resentment of Hindi is far greater than of English ... English is an essential language in India, not only because of its technical vocabularies and the international communication which it makes possible, but also simply to permit two Indians to talk together in a tongue which neither party hates.[27]

Later, in his preface to *The Vintage Book of Modern Indian Writing 1947-1997*,[28] Rushdie reaffirmed his position in the following terms:

> English has become an Indian language. Its colonial origins mean that, like Urdu and unlike all other Indian languages, it has no regional base ... English has acquired, in the South, an air of *lingua franca* cultural neutrality. The new Silicon Valley-style boom in computer technology that is transforming the economies of Bangalore and Madras has made English, in those cities, an even more important language than before.[29]

Rushdie thus implies an objectivist, non-communalist model of language use which refuses to make an automatic or emotional distinction between English on the one hand and India's longer-established languages on the other.

In a more descriptive vein, the scholar Jaydeep Sarangi, writing in 2005, identifies, using a sociolinguistic discourse, certain characteristics of Indian English thus:

> In the linguistically and culturally pluralistic Indian subcontinent English is used as the Second Language (L2), which is acquired after one has learnt the First Language (L1). This co-existence ... results in interference from one's First Language in the Second Language. Through a large-scale socio-cultural interaction with regional contexts English becomes Indianised. A variety of English albeit non-native, lexically, morphologically, syntactically, stylistically and

> sociolinguistically different from the Standard British form has come to be known as *Indian Variety of English* .... [30] English, as a link language in India, carries the weight of different experiences in different contexts/ surroundings. English is essentially malleable in nature, adapting its form to suit cultural contexts ... . [31] In the case of literary *Indian English*, *loan translations* or *word borrowings* from the regional languages of the subcontinent are embedded in the English text, as markers pointing out a cultural distinctiveness. The writers of Indian writings in English often refuse to gloss untranslated words/expressions to be true to their respective roots. *Lexical openness* is a trademark of Indian English canon. [32]

One of the most important aspects of any claim for Indian English as a major variety of International Standard of English is, clearly, the literary dimension, and in our times, the Indian capacity, as identified early by Macaulay, for "facility and correctness" of expression in English manifests itself in the multiform literary phenomenon known as Indian Writing in English / IWE. It is certainly of major significance that Indians — like other post-colonial users of English — should see that language as a valid channel not merely for business or administrative transactions but also, and abundantly, for their own creative writing: indeed, one might even put forward the creative writing factor as a litmus test for distinguishing between second-language (e.g. Indian) and foreign-language (e.g. mainland European) users of English.

India's remains a divided literary community, with permanent tensions existing along two fault-lines — writers in English versus writers in Indian languages, and expatriate versus India-based writers. Those living writers with international reputations, whether living in India or not, tend overwhelmingly to be English-medium novelists: Salman Rushdie, Vikram Seth, Vikram Chandra, Amitav Ghosh or Rohinton Mistry; Anita Desai, Kiran Desai, Jhumpa Lahiri, Arundhati Roy, Shashi Deshpande, Githa Hariharan or Manju Kapur.

IWE actually dates back to the 1830s, but even today it is no problem-free genre. Some of its inherent cruxes were perspicaciously outlined well before the current wave, in 1968 by the Calcutta-based British critic David McCutchion, who, in his pioneering volume *Indian Writing in English,* asked a set of questions which are still pertinent today: "To what extent are Indian writers in English truly bilingual? ... In so far as the Indian writer in English does write for his fellow Indians and not the overseas market, what audience does he have in mind?".[33] He adds: "The fascination of Indian writing in English lies ... in the phenomenon ... of literary creativity in a language other than the surrounding mother tongue,"[34] and highlights the particular technical difficulties raised by dialogue in IWE works: "It would require very exceptional gifts and total bilingualism to express directly in English the lives of people who do not themselves speak English,"[35] while noting the very specific positioning of the Indian intellectual writing in English: "What the Indian poet or novelist may present ... is his own experience as a man educated to think and feel in Western categories confronting the radically different culture all around him."[36] McCutchion supposes a surface-and-depth model: under the English-language surface lies a "radically different" Indian *mind*.

Bearing in mind McCutchion's still-valid comments, we may define Indian Writing in English as original creative writing produced in English by Indian writers or writers of Indian origin, resident or expatriate, for whom English will normally be a second language but who have in all probability been educated, even within India, in English-medium schools and universities, and are likely to "think and feel" in English and to write it more fluently than any Indian language. This set of conditions in no way makes these writers any less Indian: in most cases they are representing the lives, conversations and thoughts of Indian characters who more often than not are presumed to be speaking and thinking not in English at all, but in a plurality of Indian languages.

IWE remains controversial in Indian critical circles, being regarded by some as "insufficiently Indian" or "inauthentic," notably when practised by expatriates. The position continues to exist that writers in Indian languages are somehow more

"Indian" than those who write in English. Rushdie, Seth and the rest are accused by some of being out of touch, cutting themselves off from their roots, and failing to reflect the "authentic India". Thus, in a lecture of 1999, the critic Meenakshi Mukherjee said of the expatriate novelists: "these writers have to (...) exoticize the Indian landscape to signal their Indianness to the West, in the context of the Western market."[37] The expatriates, for their part, tend to defend their own practice by invoking an immanent Indian tradition of hybridity. Thus, Vikram Chandra, who happened to be the main target of Mukherjee's strictures, counter-attacked in the *Boston Review*, rejecting such "censorious rhetoric about correct Indianness" and recalling that "Indians have lived in many languages simultaneously for thousands of years."[38] The dividing-lines of language and residence are, in any case, not absolute: a poet like Jayanta Mahapatra writes in both English and Oriya, while the Bombay-based novelist Kiran Nagarkar has published novels written directly in both Marathi and English. Expatriate writers like Seth, Chandra or Ghosh all regularly spend time in India and research their novels there. Meanwhile, and if the advantages of writing in English for the international market are obvious, it is also the case that English is the only language in which an Indian novelist can be read over the entire country without having to be translated: the English-language reading public may be relatively small, but it is pan-Indian.

The language of IWE texts is recognisably the Indian variant of International Standard English, as will be shown in detail in the study that follows. IWE writers tend not to provide glossaries for the Indian lexical items that appear in their books, presuming that Indians will understand them and that other readers, Anglophone or not, will guess their general sense from context.[39] One may also note in IWE texts the interesting phenomenon of a certain linguistic indeterminacy as regards dialogue: it is often difficult for the reader to decide, or know, whether the characters are talking to each other in English or in Hindi or another Indian language, and in many cases one might conclude that only the author knows. Further, in the themes treated in their fiction

IWE writers often display a keen awareness of the complexities of language issues. Anita Desai's *In Custody* (1984) is an elegy for the post-Independence decline of Urdu language and culture; Ghosh's *The Hungry Tide* (2004) has as its protagonist and prime mover a professional translator-interpreter, conversant in six languages; Chandra's *Sacred Games* (2006) offers an English strewn with Indian words and expressions in a dozen or more Indian languages, plus Arabic and a hybrid "Bombay slang". Seth's epic *A Suitable Boy* (1993), a text which will be looked at in detail by Sumana Bandyopadhyay, interweaves characters who would in reality have spoken variously in Hindi, Urdu, Bengali and English, and in numerous episodes highlights the tensions between those languages. Thus, in Seth's novel, a Bengali poet reads from his work to the local literary society; a woman in the audience asks him: "Why is it that you do not write in Bengali, your mother tongue?"; the poet's answer is that "his Bengali was not good enough for him to be able to express himself in the manner he could in English," and he adds that "even Sanskrit came to India from outside."[40] All in all, we may conclude that IWE as a genre is a fully engaged element in the rich and dynamic multilingual reality of today's India.

* * * * * * * *

The present study by Sumana Bandyopadhyay is a significant new contribution to the understanding of both Indian English and IWE in the complex and evolving context we have outlined above. The author brings together diverse strands of both linguistic and literary scholarship, laying particular stress on how Indian English has adapted to homegrown realities while remaining a major variant of a world language. The basic position that both underlies and emerges from this study is — in consonance with the general arguments we have advanced above — that there is an Indian Standard English which is a variety of International Standard English.

This is a corpus-based analysis, and the various aspects of Indian English discussed are illustrated with examples drawn from some of the best-known living practitioners of IWE. The time-span chosen is essentially the period opened up in 1981 by Salman Rushdie's epoch-making novel *Midnight's Children*. Thus, the works of the preceding IWE generation, as famously represented by the triad of "old masters" Mulk Raj Anand, Raja Rao and R.K. Narayan, are not included in the corpus as such, although some reference is made to them across the study. The writers chosen, eight in number, for the corpus proper are (male): Salman Rushdie, Vikram Seth, Vikram Chandra, Rohinton Mistry, Amitav Ghosh, Upamanyu Chatterjee and (female): Manju Kapur and Arundhati Roy. Of these, the two women writers and Chatterjee are India-resident and the rest are expatriates (although expatriation is best seen as a relative concept, if we remember that Seth and Chandra, for instance, are both authors of major novels — *A Suitable Boy* and *Sacred Games* — researched by them in great detail in India).

The author precedes her corpus analysis with an overview of the positions on Indian English of twelve leading linguistic authorities, of whom nine are Indian and the rest — reflecting the global interest in this variant of English — from outside India. A number of themes are recurrent: Indian English as a nativised, acculturated or transplanted phenomenon; the circumstance that Indians almost always learn their English from other Indians and may have little or no contact with native speakers; the influence of Indian languages, as manifested in syntactic choices, lexical calques, or code-mixing; and the relatively formal nature of Indian English arising from the tendency not to use English in more informal situations. Considerable stress is laid on the differences at all levels between Indian and native-speaker English (e.g. dropping or addition of articles; "would" for "will"; the all-purpose "isn't it?", etc.) — to the point indeed where one author, S.K. Verma, is cited as seeing Indian English forms as examples not of "deviance" but of "creation".

The corpus analysis offered in the light of the above theoretical survey takes in aspects of Indian English on the phonological, lexical, functional and structural levels. The phonological aspect is examined with the help of Rohinton Mistry's novel *Such a Long Journey*: it is shown how Mistry's text phonetically represents Indian phonological variants (e.g.

"risvard seat" for "reserved seat"; "snack" pronounced as if "snake"). Fictional conversations excerpted from the same novel are also employed to exemplify Indian English intonation patterns. On the lexical level, the stress is on Indianisation of vocabulary (direct imports of words from Indian languages, hybrid compounds, loan-translations, etc.). Of particular interest here are the author's intelligent use of the still eminently valuable nineteenth-century work *Hobson-Jobson: The Anglo-Indian Dictionary*,[41] and her comprehensive and carefully-worked glossary of Indian lexical items in Seth's *A Suitable Boy* — a labour of love in itself from which many readers and scholars should benefit. The discussion of functional aspects prioritises such factors as the frequency of repetition in Indian English and creative coinage of expressions (with a useful glance at Arundhati Roy's facility in this respect), in an analysis drawing on sociolinguistics and pragmatics. In addition, the incidence of the "cognitive group" of verbs — such as "know," "discover," "recognise" — is examined on the basis of a number of novels from the corpus, with Ghosh to the fore (with additional examples, for the sake of comparison, from two recent British novels): the author argues from this evidence in favour of the status of Indian English as a variant of International Standard English.

* * * * * * * *

Sumana Bandyopadhyay concludes her study by stressing, with the above multifarious examples behind her, the vital and dynamic Indianness of today's Indian English as handled by IWE writers. Moving the debate on to a broader theoretical plane, she evokes Rushdie's notion of "chutneyfication," as well as Franz Fanon's concept of the "fighting phase" of the native intellectual. The question readers of this book may wish to ask themselves might well be: where are Indian English and IWE now heading? — this of course in the new and changed context of India's rise to global influence in the economic, technological and cultural spheres. If there is a new "fighting phase" for Indian English and its literary practitioners, how is the combat going to manifest itself?

IWE in some of its more recent productions — as in Anita Desai's *The Zigzag Way* (2004) with its Mexican location, Seth's non-fiction work *Two Lives* (2005) spanning India, Germany and the UK, or Rushdie's *Shalimar the Clown* (2005), which articulates globalisation's reach by encompassing Kashmir, France and the USA — now seems to be operating at an increasingly cosmopolitan level, with "Indianness" as but one of its multiple signifieds (or even absent altogether), and yet at the same time and given its writers' never-denied origins, embodying a distinctive Indian perspective on today's global realities. Meanwhile, a work like Amitav Ghosh's novel *The Hungry Tide* (2004), from a rather different perspective, has explored the competing claims of the global and the local and attempted some kind of resolution. Precisely how Indian English (as well as IWE) will position itself in a new "fighting phase" around the multiple centres of the evolving world economy remains a future wide open for active shaping by those who speak and write it. Here, Sumana Bandyopadhyay's study, wide-ranging, exploratory and suitably detailed, deserves to be hailed by its readers as part of the very necessary process of opening up new paths for research in a linguistic and cultural area which will increasingly be of concern to scholars in the humanities, both in India and in the new globalised universe as a whole.

Notes

1. A wealth of information on Indian language issues is available at the website of the electronic journal *Language in India:* www.languageinindia.com/ (see, for instance, the Hohenthal and Mallikarjun articles cited below). This site also has links to the census and constitutional material cited in this foreword, and to Macaulay's "Minute on Indian Education" (*cf.* below).
2. The languages featured on the banknotes are English and Hindi on the front, plus, on the back, 15 of the scheduled languages (Assamese, Bengali, Gujarati, Kannada, Kashmiri, Konkani, Malayalam, Marathi, Nepali, Oriya, Punjabi, Sanskrit, Tamil, Telugu and Urdu).
3. See Office of the Registrar General, India, *Census of India 1991* (Internet reference). The data regarding languages from the 2001

census did not appear to have been released at the time of writing.

4. The 1991 census lists what then numbered 18 scheduled languages. The Ninety Second Amendment was proposed in 2003 and passed in 2004 under *The Constitution (Ninety Second Amendment) Act*. See: B. Mallikarjun, "An Exploration into Linguistic Majority-Minority Relations in India" (Internet reference); and Ninety-Second Amendment text at: <http://indiacode.nic.in/coiweb/amend/amend92.htm>.
5. For detailed information on the main Indian languages (number of speakers, where spoken, script), see the website Major Indian Languages [no author cited; reference in Works Cited], http://theory.tifr.res.in/bombay/history/people/language/; also Andrew Dalby, *Dictionary of Languages*.
6. See Constitution of India (Internet reference).
7. See Official Languages Act 1963 (Internet reference).
8. David Graddol, "The Decline of the Native Speaker," 159-160.
9. Tom McArthur, *Oxford Guide to World English*, 312.
10. See Census of India 1991, www.censusindia.net/cendat/language/lang1.html, and: Asunción Moreno *et al.*, "Collection of SLR in the Asian-Pacific area," 2004, http://lands.let.kun.nl/literature/heuvel.2004.2.pdf (SLR = Spoken Language Resources).
11. Annika Hohenthal, "English in India" (Internet reference).
12. B. Mallikarjun, "Fifty Years of Language Planning" (Internet reference).
13. Statistics from Government of India, Department of Education site (Internet reference). The figures correspond to the books received over the period by the National Library of Calcutta (Kolkata), a copyright library under the Delivery of Books Act.
14. N. Ram, "The Great Indian Media Bazaar," 253.
15. Ram, "The Great Indian Media Bazaar," 253.
16. See http://en.wikipedia.org/wiki/The_Times_of_India: "*The Times of India* ... has the highest circulation amongst English language daily broadsheets in the world."
17. Ram, "The Great Indian Media Bazaar," 255.
18. Since 1999 Chandra Bhan Prasad has been the author of a weekly column on Dalit issues in Delhi's long-established newspaper *The Pioneer*. His columns are collected in *Dalit Diary: 1999-2003: Reflections on Apartheid in India* (see Works Cited).
19. Chandra Bhan Prasad, "The 'impure' milk of Lord Macaulay," *The Pioneer*, 3 December 2000; in *Dalit Diary*, 92-94 (93, 94).
20. Thomas Babington Macaulay, "Minute on Indian Education" (Internet reference).

21. Michael Madhusudan Dutt, "The Anglo-Saxon and the Hindu," 6.
22. Bankim Chandra Chatterjee, "A Popular Literature for Bengal," 14.
23. Raja Rao, *Kanthapura* , 5.
24. A.K. Ramanujan, "Is There An Indian Way of Thinking?", 437.
25. Shashi Deshpande, *The Dark Holds No Terrors,* 150.
26. Vikram Chandra, *Red Earth and Pouring Rain*, 344. NB: the editions of novels cited in this foreword and in Sumana Bandyopadhyay's book are not necessarily the same.
27. Salman Rushdie, 'Commonwealth literature' does not exist", 65-66.
28. The anthology is co-edited by Rushdie and Elizabeth West; the preface is by Rushdie.
29. Rushdie, "Preface" to Rushdie and West (eds.), *The Vintage Book of Modern Indian Writing 1947-1997*, xiii.
30. Jaydeep Sarangi, *Indian Novels in English: A Sociolinguistic Study*, 17.
31. Sarangi, *Indian Novels in English*, 18.
32. Sarangi, *Indian Novels in English*, 19.
33. David McCutchion, "Introduction" [1968] to *Indian Writing in English: A Collection of Critical Essays*, 22.
34. McCutchion, *Indian Writing in English*, 10.
35. McCutchion, *Indian Writing in English*, 15.
36. McCutchion, *Indian Writing in English*, 16.
37. Meenakshi Mukherjee (1999), quoted in Vikram Chandra, "The Cult of Authenticity: India's cultural commissars worship 'Indianness' instead of art," (Internet reference).
38. Chandra, "The Cult of Authenticity."
39. Translators of IWE into other Western languages do, however, often provide glossaries.
40. Vikram Seth, *A Suitable Boy*, 1369.
41. Compiled by Henry Yule and A.C. Burnell in 1886 (see Works Cited).

Works Cited

Anderman, Gunilla and Margaret Rogers (eds.). *Translation Today: Trends and Perspectives*. Clevedon, England: Multilingual Matters, 2003.

Chandra, Vikram. "The Cult of Authenticity: India's cultural commissars worship 'Indianness' instead of art". *Boston Review* (1999), http://bostonreview.mit.edu/BR25.1/chandra.html.

Chandra, Vikram. *Red Earth and Pouring Rain* [1995]. London: Faber & Faber, 1996.

Chandra, Vikram. *Sacred Games*. London: Faber & Faber, 2006.

Chatterjee, Bankim Chandra. 'A Popular Literature for Bengal' [1870]. In Chaudhuri, Amit (ed.). *The Picador Book of Modern Indian Literature*. London: Picador, 2001, 113-119.

Chaudhuri, Amit (ed.). *The Picador Book of Modern Indian Literature*. London: Picador, 2001.

Constitution of India, <http://indiacode.nic.in/coiweb/welcome.html>.

Dalby, Andrew. *Dictionary of Languages*. London: Bloomsbury, 1998, rev. 2004.

Department of Education (India), www.education.nic.in/htmlweb/cr_piracy_study/cpr6.htm.

Desai, Anita. *In Custody*. [1984]. London: Vintage, 1999.

Desai, Anita. *The Zigzag Way*. London: Chatto & Windus, 2004.

Deshpande, Shashi. *The Dark Holds No Terrors*. [1980]. New Delhi: Penguin, 1990.

Dutt, Michael Madhusudan. "The Anglo-Saxon and the Hindu" [1854]. Excerpted in Chaudhuri, Amit (ed.). *The Picador Book of Modern Indian Literature*. London: Picador, 2001, 5-7.

Ghosh, Amitav. *The Hungry Tide*. London: Harper Collins, 2004.

Graddol, David. "The Decline of the Native Speaker". In Gunilla Anderman and Margaret Rogers (eds.). *Translation Today: Trends and Perspectives*. Clevedon, England: Multilingual Matters, 2003, 152-167.

Hohenthal, Annika. "English in India: Loyalty and Attitudes". Language in India Vol. 3:5, May 2003. www.languageinindia.com/may2003/annika.html.

Macaulay, Thomas Babington. "Minute on Indian Education" [1835]. Singapore: National University of Singapore, 2003, www.scholars.nus.edu.sg/literature/macaulay.html.

Major Indian Languages [website; no author cited], http://theory.tifr.res.in/bombay/history/people/language/.

Mallikarjun, B. "An Exploration into Linguistic Majority-Minority Relations in India". *Language in India*, Vol. 4:8, August 2004, www.languageinindia.com/aug2004/dlamallikarjun2.html.

Mallikarjun, B. "Fifty Years of Language Planning for Modern Hindi". *Language in India*,Vol. 4:11, November 2004, www.languageinindia.com/nov2004/mallikarjunmalaysiapaper1.html.

McArthur, Tom. *Oxford Guide to World English*. Oxford: OUP, 2002.

McCutchion, David. *Indian Writing in English: A Collection of Critical Essays*. Calcutta: Writers Workshop. 1969, repr. 1997.

Mistry, Rohinton. *Such A Long Journey*. New Delhi: Penguin. 2002.

Moreno, Asunción *et al*. "Collection of SLR in the Asian-Pacific area". 2004. http://lands.let.kun.nl/literature/heuvel.2004.2.pdf.

Office of the Registrar General : *Census of India 1991*, www.censusindia.net/.

Official Languages Act, 1963, www.languageinindia.com/april2002/officiallanguagesact.html.

Prasad, Chandra Bhan. *Dalit Diary: 1999-2003: Reflections on Apartheid in India*. Pondicherry: Navayana, 2004.

Ram, N. "The Great Indian Media Bazaar". In Romila Thapar, ed. *India: Another Millennium?* [2000]. New Delhi: Penguin, 2001, 241-292.

Ramanujan, A.K. "Is There An Indian Way of Thinking?: An Informal Essay" [1989]. In Chaudhuri, Amit (ed.). *The Picador Book of Modern Indian Literature*. London: Picador, 2001, 420-437.

Rao, Raja. *Kanthapura* [1938]. New Delhi: Orient Paperbacks, 2001.

Rushdie, Salman. " 'Commonwealth literature' does not exist" [1983]. In *Imaginary Homelands*. London: Granta, 1992, 61-70.

Rushdie, Salman. "Preface" to Salman Rushdie and Elizabeth West (eds.). *The Vintage Book of Modern Indian Writing 1947-1997*. London: Vintage, 1997, ix-xxiii.

Rushdie, Salman. *Midnight's Children*. London: Jonathan Cape, 1981.

Rushdie, Salman. *Shalimar the Clown*. New York: Random House, 2005.

Sarangi, Jaydeep. *Indian Novels in English: A Sociolinguistic Study*. Bareilly: Prakash Book Depot, 2005.

Seth, Vikram. *A Suitable Boy* [1993]. London: Phoenix, 1994.

Seth, Vikram. *Two Lives*. London: Little, Brown, 2005.

Thapar, Romila, ed. *India: Another Millennium?* [2000]. New Delhi: Penguin, 2001.

Yule, Henry and A.C. Burnell. *Hobson-Jobson: The Anglo-Indian Dictionary*. [1886]. Ware, England: Wordsworth Editions. 1996.

15th November 2007.

Preface

"Indian English" is an overarching term that refers to various forms of English used in India. It has the status of an Indian language, serves the international, intra-national and intra-regional roles of communication among people of diverse linguistic backgrounds. From the vantage position of the linguist, Indian Writing in English offers rich data for analysis. In the past, writers as V. K. Gokak, Ramesh Mohan, S. K. Verma, and Braj B. Kachru defined the process of Indianisation of English based on the data collected from earlier Indian English fictional and journalistic writings. This study is concerned with the linguistic analysis of Indianisation of English grounded on its use in contemporary Indian English fiction from the year 1980 to 2005. The bilingual authors selected for the study have English as their second language and are taken to represent the four regions of India. Accordingly, Vikram Seth and Salman Rushdie stand for the north, Rohinton Mistry for the west, Amitav Ghosh and Upamanyu Chatterjee for the east and Arundhati Roy for the south. Besides these, other authors taken up in the study are Manju Kapur and Vikram Chandra. Since the topic of the research is Indianisation of English, the works that are wholly or partly about India, with the sole exception of *An Equal Music*, are included in the analysis. This study was undertaken to find out certain aspects of Indianness of Indian English at the levels of Phonology, Morphology, Syntax, and Semantics. It investigates the domains in which Indian English tends to be used and highlights the linguistic aspects of its form. In order to accomplish the objectives of the study, the data was collected from selected fictional writings of the authors mentioned above.

The book is divided into seven chapters. The first chapter,

"Introduction," describes the process of Indianisation of English. It deals with the definition of Indian English, its domains, registers, and characteristics. The second chapter, "Review of Literature," presents an overview of the findings of a number of scholars. These scholars focused on the lexicon, phonology, word formation, and syntactic features of Indian English corpus found in the domains of education, government administration, and media. The third chapter, "Phonological Features," presents the phonological features represented in the orthography of Indian English fiction. This chapter is concerned with pronunciation, phonetics, phonology, and intonation of Indian English. The different functions of intonation discussed are attitudinal function, discourse function, and grammatical function. The fourth chapter entitled "Lexical Features" discusses the lexical features of Indian English and includes kinds of borrowing and classification of Indian words and expressions in Indian English fiction of the nineteen eighties and nineties. The thrust is on the borrowed words in Vikram Seth's *A Suitable Boy* and Salman Rushdie's *Midnight's Children*. The semantic changes in word formation found in the works of other authors are discussed under generalization, specialisation, transference, and degeneration. A special section analyses in detail the interjection *arrey*.

The fifth chapter entitled "Functional Features" aims at discussing exclusively the functional features of Indian English under three categories, namely, repetition, cliché, and Indianisms. The phenomena of repetition found in conversational extracts from Vikram Seth's *An Equal Music* are associated with some clusters of verbs. Six different categories are analysed under cliché. The section on Indianisms is a study on Rohinton Mistry's novel, *A Fine Balance*. The sixth chapter, "Structural Features," deals with some structural features of Indian English. This chapter includes the semantic structures of the verbs preceding complementisers and a syntactic discussion of complementisers from four novels of Amitav Ghosh. Syntactic correlates of semantic features are also analysed. Finally, the seventh chapter,

"Conclusion," contains brief summaries of the chapters and limitations of the work undertaken. Each of the seven chapters concludes with its respective findings. Interesting findings come out of the study in relation to vowel changes in consonantal environments, nominal borrowings and use of common words across authors despite different L1 influences, repetition as a major feature in conversational extracts, *that* complementiser's dominant and frequent occurrence, comparatively sparse *wh*-complementiser, and certain linguistic factors determining the Indianness of Indian English.

The novels chosen for the work were written in the time span from the 1980s to 2005. The work focused on authors who had started their careers in the last two decades, and whose writings were considered as canonical Indian writing in English (IWE). There was a north-west-east-south categorisation of the subcontinent where an author whose writings had gained wide acclamation in the literary world had been chosen from each of the regions. The works of these authors were discussed in the following paragraphs.

Arundhati Roy's *The God of Small Things* published in 1997, won the Booker Prize in the same year and had been translated into twenty seven languages. Her other writings, such as *The Algebra of Infinite Justice* (2002), *Public Power in the Age of Empire* (2004), *The Cost of Living* (1999), *War is Peace* (2001), *Power Politics* (2001) and others were non-fiction. Upamanyu Chatterjee's *English, August : An Indian Story* (1988), *The Last Burden* (1993), *The Mammaries of the Welfare State* (2000), *Weight Loss* (2006), were scanned for analysis. Dev Benegal made *English, August : An Indian Story* into a film in 1994. The fiction was a critical and popular success outside India. The two Agastya Sen novels, published in 1988 and 2000, focused on the life of a young Indian bureaucrat, were also scanned for the study. Chatterjee was the first of the present generation Indian authors to find success outside India.

Vikram Seth's novels taken for the study were *A Suitable Boy* (1993) and *An Equal Music* (1999). *A Suitable Boy* with

1349 pages was the largest single volume novel ever published in English. The novel was chosen for the Commonwealth Writers Prize and W. H. Smith Literary Award in 1994. It was short listed for Irish Times International Fiction Prize in 1993. BT Ethnic and Multicultural Media Award selected *An Equal Music* as the best book in 2001. Seth received Pravasi Bharatiya Samman in 2006 for his exceptional and meritorious contribution as a writer. Seth's *Two lives* (2005), is a non-fiction family memoir. It is about the lives of his great uncle (Shanti Bihari Seth) and his German-Jewish great aunt (Henny Caro). *The Golden Gate* (1986), is a novel in verse, composed in tetrameter sonnets.

Amitav Ghosh's *The Circle of Reason* (1986), *The Shadow lines* (1988), *The Calcutta Chromosome* (1996) and *The Hungry Tide* (2004) were taken up for the study. *The Calcutta Chromosome* was awarded Puscart Prize in 1999 and Arthur C. Clark award in 1997. Ghosh received the Sahitya Akademi Award, India's prestigious literary prize for *The Shadow Lines.* The work had been translated into Hindi and Urdu. His *Dancing in Cambodia, at Large in Burma* (1998) and *Countdown* (1999) (composed on India's nuclear policy) are non-fiction. His other novel, *The Glass Palace* (2000) was not included in the study.

Rohinton Mistry's *Such a Long Journey* (1992) and *A Fine Balance* (1996) were awarded the Commonwealth Writers prizes. *Tales from Firozsha Baag* is a collection of short stories, and so did not fit the scheme of this study. Other fictions analysed were Manju Kapur's *Difficult Daughters* (1998), and Vikram Chandra's *Red Earth* and *Pouring Rain* (1995). The Commonwealth Prize Committee nominated both of them as the best first book. Chandra's *Love and Longing in Bombay* (1998) received the Commonwealth Writers prize in 1998. The other novel in the study was Salman Rushdie's *Midnight's Children.* The fiction was awarded the Booker Prize in 1981 and the Booker of Bookers in 1992.

Frantz Fanon in his significant study on the effects of colonisation in *The Wretched of the Earth,* discussed three phases of reclamation of non-native writers. According to him, the first phase was the period of unqualified assimilation. In this period, the native intellectual assimilates the culture of the occupying power. In the second phase, the native writer decides to recollect and represent his ancient culture. His creative work is then composed of old legends reinterpreted in the light of a borrowed aestheticism. The third phase for Fanon was the fighting phase. During this phase, the native intellectual turns himself into an awakener of the people. According to Fanon, this phase is crucial since a great many men and women feel the need to speak to their nation, to compose the sentence that expresses the heart of the people and to become the mouthpiece of a new reality in action. Hence a fighting literature, a revolutionary literature, and a national literature with a distinct voice come into existence.

Applying Fanon's distinction of the three phases of reclamation to study Indianisation of English, the following categories can be discussed. The first phase of Indian Writing in English dates back to 1830s, to Kashiprasad Ghosh, the first Indian poet writing in English. However in the beginning, political writing dominated the literary world. Rammohun Roy wrote about social reform and religion in English. The earlier generation of writers, particularly Raja Rao, Mulk Raj Anand and R.K. Narayan can be classified under the second phase of the evolution. Raja Rao in *Kanthapura* brings out from the depths of his memory the past happenings of the bygone days. The works of the Indian authors writing in English considered for this study can be categorised in the third phase of evolution which characterises the distinctive works of native writers. In India, creative writing in English is considered as an integral part of the national literatures.

This book is essentially a revised and extended version of my Ph.D. dissertation.

I am grateful to Dr. T. Ravichandran of the I.I.T., Kanpur for the encouragement and care, suggestions and criticisms during the preparation of this work. I am indebted to my teachers, Prof. B.N. Patnaik, now at the Central Institute of Indian Languages, Mysore, Prof. Achla M. Raina, Prof. G. Neelakantan, Dr. Mini Chandran, Dr. Suchitra Mathur, and Prof. Bijoy H. Baruah. I have also benefited from the lectures of Prof. Harish Karnick and Prof. Amitabh Mukherjee of the Computer Science and Engineering, I.I.T., Kanpur and Prof. Krishna Bhattacharya of the Calcutta University, and from discussions with my father Dr. S. N. Banerjee, formerly of the Department of Humanities and Social Sciences, I.I.T., Kharagpur.

I owe special thanks to Dr. Christopher Rollason of Metz, France for his Foreword to this book.

To my mother Smt. Shakuntala Banerjee and sister, Smt. Anurai Banerjee, I would like to express my appreciation for their support and understanding. I am much obliged to my maternal uncle Dr. Amitava Mukherjee, who inspired me to publish this work.

I thank Mr. Ashok Kumar Mittal, of Concept Publishing Company Pvt. Ltd., my publisher, for all his help and suggestions.

Kolkata **Dr. Sumana Bandyopadhyay**
15th August 2009

A Note on Documentation

- The book is closely formatted in adherence to Joseph Gibaldi's *MLA Handbook for Writers of Research Papers: Sixth Edition,* New Delhi: Affiliated East-West Press, 2004.
- Standard British spelling is followed throughout the main text. However, American spellings inside quotations or newly introduced terms are retained.
- For novels in which there are frequent references, the following abbreviations are used:

Amitav Ghosh:

TCOR : *The Circle of Reason* (New Delhi: Ravi Dayal Publisher, 2003).

TSL : *The Shadow Lines* (New Delhi: Ravi Dayal Publisher, 2003).

TCC : *The Calcutta Chromosome* (New Delhi: Ravi Dayal Publisher, 2005).

THT : *The Hungry Tide* (New Delhi: Harper Collins Publishers, 2005).

Arundhati Roy:

TGOST : *The God of Small Things* (New Delhi: Penguin, 2002).

Manju Kapur:

DD : *Difficult Daughters* (New Delhi: Penguin, 1998).

Rohinton Mistry:

SALJ : *Such a Long Journey* (Noida: Penguin Books, 2002).

AFB : *A Fine Balance* (Noida: Penguin Books, 2003).

Salman Rushdie:

M's C : *Midnight's Children* (London: Vintage, 1995).

Upamanyu Chatterjee:

EA : English, August : An Indian Story (New Delhi : Penguin Books, 2002).

TLB : *The Last Burden* (London: Faber and Faber, 1993).

Vikram Chandra:

LALIB : *Love and Longing in Bombay* (Boston: Little Brown and Company, 1997).

Vikram Seth:

AEM : *An Equal Music* (New Delhi: Penguin Books, 2000).

ASB : *A Suitable Boy* (New Delhi: Penguin Books, 2003).

List of Phonetic Symbols

/ i /	=	front high vowel
/ I /	=	centered front high vowel
/ e/	=	mid-high front vowel
/ æ /	=	mid-low front vowel
/ *x* /	=	mid-low front vowel
/ a /	=	front low vowel
/ ⊃ /	=	mid-low back vowel
/ o /	=	mid-high back vowel
/ u /	=	back high vowel
/ ʋ /	=	centered back high vowel
/ ъ /	=	back low vowel
/ ə /	=	central vowel
/ ɜ /	=	mid central vowel
/ ʌ /	=	central low vowel
/ b /	=	bilabial voiced plosive
/ ph /	=	bilabial aspirated stop
/ t /	=	alveolar voiceless plosive
/ d /	=	alveolar voiced plosive
/ T /	=	retroflex voiceless plosive
/ D /	=	retroflex voiced plosive
/ f /	=	labio-dental voiceless fricative
/ v /	=	labio-dental voiced fricative
/ ⊘ /	=	dental voiceless fricative
/ ð /	=	dental voiced fricative
/ s /	=	alveolar voiceless fricative
/ z /	=	alveolar voiced fricative
/ ʃ /	=	palato-alveolar voiceless fricative
/ ǯ /	=	palato-alveolar voiced fricative
/ tʃ /	=	palato-alveolar voiceless affricate
/ dǯ /	=	palato-alveolar voiced affricate

/ ŋ /	=	velar nasal
/ l /	=	lateral
/ r /	=	post-alveolar frictionless continuant
/ j /	=	unrounded palatal semi-vowel
/ w /	=	labio-velar semi-vowel

Contents

Chapter -1

Introduction

The origin and growth of Indian English as a means of communication primarily between the Indians and the British administrators and officials of the East India Company posted in the subcontinent and later on among Indians (with various L1s) themselves can be evaluated from documents[1] of the late seventeenth century onwards. In this chapter, Indian English is considered under the following heads:

1. Indianisation of English
2. Indian English : Definition, Domains, and Characteristics
3. Registers of Indian English
4. Linguistic Analysis of Indian English Literature
5. The Origins of Indian English
6. Some Aspects of Style and Language in Earlier Indian English Fiction
7. English in India
8. Findings

1. Indianisation of English

In India, the English language by degrees became a symbol of political power. Gradually it came to be the language of the legal system, higher education, administrative network, science and technology, trade and commerce—either because the indigenous languages were not equipped for these roles or English provided a convenient vocabulary, or because the use of English was considered prestigious and powerful. The process of Indianisation of English is both due to transfer from local languages as well as to the new cultural environment and communicative needs (Saghal, "Patterns of Language Use" 300). Because of social penetration and the extended range of functions of English in diverse sociolinguistic contexts there are several varieties, localised registers and genres for articulating local, social, cultural, and religious identities (Kachru, "World Englishes" 69).

English in India has come far from its original uses in the colonial times when it was generally used as the language of the government. Now-a-days, English has spread into many new domains including the more personal ones such as the family and friendship. English has also acquired new functions like the self-expression or innovative function. In the neighbourhood domain, English is the most preferred option when people's languages differ. In the areas of education, government, and employment, English shows itself without doubt as by far the most preferred medium.

2. Indian English : Definition, Domains, and Characteristics

The term "Indian English" refers to the variety of English, which is learnt and, used by a large number of educated (i.e. in the conventional sense, someone who has undergone an intellectual and moral training) Indians as a second language. Indian English is a cover term, which refers to forms of English used in India. There are three hundred and thirty three million users[2] in India. Indian English has the status of an Indian language, serves the international role of medium of communication with the global community of nations and intra-national and intra-regional roles of link language among people of diverse linguistic backgrounds.

Similar descriptive terms have been used to refer to other non-native varieties of English such as Sri Lankan English, Singapore English and Nigerian English. The native varieties of English are American English, Canadian English, British English, Australian English and New Zealand English.

Indian English is a product of contact between English and Indian mother tongues of the bilinguals who use it. An ideal bilingual is one who is capable of using two languages with equal ease in every situation. When an Indian uses English in India, the speech shares many of the features of the other Indian codes with which English alternates. Indian English thus deviates from the norms of native varieties of English. This deviation is a natural sequence of social conditions in the immediate environment in which the language is spoken. This linguistic interference is phonological, grammatical and lexical. Attempts have, however, been made to standardise spoken Indian English for pedagogical purposes, a pan-Indian neutral variety of spoken English called "General Indian English" (GIE) is recommended for purposes of teaching in schools and colleges. The L1 (first language) interference is not restricted to the level of phonology; it is found in lexis, collocations and transfer of idioms from Indian languages in Indian English.

Attempts have been made since the nineteenth century to list Indian lexical items in Indian English. Scholars such as Yule and Burnell in 1886, Wilson in 1885, Subba Rao in 1954 had done this. Later on, an appendix of the *Oxford Advance Learner's Dictionary* 1996, supplies a list of Indian words used in English, though the list is yet to join the main entries and be accepted as "standard" English. Kachru notes in this context that a dictionary of Indian English is " . . . basically a dictionary of English with an added dimension of area-bound, context-bound and language-bound features which separate the Indian variety of English from others" (*Indianisation* 169). In addition to linguistic interference from the Indian languages, other factors, which contribute to the identity of Indian English as a variety, are social and cultural contexts. The nature of the language is related to the functions it serves. Although English was an alien language in India, over the years it has blended with the cultural and social matrix of the region and thus has become Indianised through a long process of acculturation.

According to Kachru, "In India an *idiom* of English has developed which is Indian in the sense that there are formal and contextual exponents of Indianness in such writing, and the *defining context* of such idiom is the Indian setting" ("The Indianness" 396). For him, several Indian English expressions were used which are deviants from the point of view of the native speaker of the language. Indian English chiefly functions in the Indian sociolinguistic context. The speech community consists of those bilinguals who use it as a second language in the Indian social, educational, literary, and administrative contexts. The specific functions for the use of English in India are of formal rather than informal or intimate. Raja Rao rightly observes that "It [English] is the language of our intellectual make-up—like Sanskrit or Persian was before—but not of our emotional make up" (*Kanthapura* 5). Today, Indian English is much more interesting and much freer than it used to be.

The conditions of learning and teaching English in India are different from the places where it is acquired as a native language. English is not acquired but learnt as L2 in a formal classroom situation, where the Indian teachers themselves speak and write Indian English. Since the majority of the Indians use English to communicate with other Indians in typically Indian situations, the desire to communicate, to put the message across overrides the desire to approximate one's language with the native speaker's English. Once a phonological, grammatical pattern or a lexical item can communicate adequately the desired meaning then there is little motivation to learn the native pattern or item. Kachru mentions that since the 1940s, English has become a part of the linguistic resources of the country, the salient features of which can be mentioned as: (1) English has the status of an 'associate' official language recognised by the Constitution, (2) India is the third largest English using nation, (3) It is the state language of Manipur, Meghalaya, Nagaland, and Tripura, and (4) It is the medium of instruction in education (*Indianization* 71).

3. Registers of Indian English

Indian English is an overarching term for a variety of Englishes used in India as a second language. In a second language variety, there are different levels of language proficiency. The Indian English speech community comprises, on the one hand, highly educated people whose command of English is near-native, and on the other hand, diverse people whose overall competence in English is negligible but can use the language in their restricted spheres of activity, for example, waiters, tourist guides and shopkeepers. There are other educated Indians in between—administrators, teachers, business executives, scientists, and journalists—who use English in a variety of professional and social situations. Educated Indian English is the English of these people. This range of Indian English has been described in literature by employing the concept of "cline"[3] —an arbitrary scale—of bilinguals with the ambilingual, the central and the zero point (Halliday, *et al.*, "The Linguistic Sciences"; Kachru "The Indianness," "Indian English"; Verma "The Systemicness of Indian English," "Syntactic Irregularities"; S. N. Sridhar "Toward a Syntax"). This study is concerned with the educated variety of Indian English in which literary works have been composed from the 1980s till 2005.

The regional varieties of Indian English have been referred to earlier. At the lexical and syntactical level, there does not seem to be much difference between these regional varieties. Another parameter, which is important in differentiating between varieties, is the use of language in certain specific situations to perform certain specific tasks. Since English is being used for many years in different situations, several registers of Indian English have developed; for example, the registers of the legal system, administration, business, finance, science and technology, Indian philosophy, art, criticism, creative writing, advertising, and so on. An investigation into these several registral varieties will provide an insight into societal functions and range of Indian English.

4. Linguistic Analysis of Indian English Literature

Previously, studies carried on Indian English had concentrated more on literary forms than on linguistic aspects. A notable example is the Bibliography[4] of Indian English prepared by the Central Institute of English and Foreign Languages in 1988 that has 1847 entries in its Indian English literature section as against 159 entries in its Indian English language section. These 159 entries include phonological, syntactic, and lexical analyses and dictionaries of Indian English. In recent years, Indian English literature has grown in various literary forms, for example, fiction, poetry, essays and biographies, and contrary to the earlier carping attitude and criticism, Indian English writing has been accepted and recognised. This study is concerned with the creative use of English by Indian English writers, particularly, the fictionists as Vikram Seth, Rohinton Mistry, Amitav Ghosh, Arundhati Roy, Salman Rushdie, Vikram Chandra, Upamanyu Chatterjee and Manju Kapur. From the linguist's point of view, Indian Writing in English offers rich data. Linguistic studies of English corpus have mostly concentrated on registral, stylistic, collocational, semantic and lexical features, which distinguish it from writing in native varieties of English. For instance, the works by Rubdy, Sridhar, Kachru and Parasher deal with these aspects.

As pointed out by Kachru in his article "Models for Non-Native Englishes," literary creativity can be viewed as a framework for "contact literatures" where in some cases, the historical and cultural presuppositions are Indian. There is cohesion of the discourse devices of other languages of the bilingual Indian writer. The bilingualism of the creative writer provides a linguistic resource and native similes and metaphors result from combinations of words.

It is evident from the literature that Mulk Raj Anand, Khushwant Singh and Salman Rushdie and other contemporary authors used transcreated speech acts from Indian languages and Raja Rao made use of culturally appropriate speech styles (Kachru, "Indian English" 32). The creative writers in Indian

English, particularly after the 1970s, experimented with the bilingual and the bicultural competence of the reader in creating a hybrid identity that is typically and multiculturally Indian.

5. The Origins of Indian English

The English language, because of its long use in India, is the associate official language and a link language among different linguistic communities in the country. The language spoken and written in India, does not basically differ from British English and American English. The spoken and written Indian English is usually intelligible internationally. R. K. Bansal writes: "English as spoken by educated people in India does not differ radically from native English in grammar and vocabulary. It is in pronunciation that Indian English is different from either British or American English" (*Spoken English* 96-97). As English in India has to meet the needs of its users, it has developed its own regional and class varieties. However, in spite of such dialectal variations, today there is an educated variety of Indian English, the Standard Indian English, which is taught in schools and universities and used in the media and by all Indian writers.

According to Zacharias Thundy ("The Origins of Indian English" 30), phonetic features of Indian English resemble American English more than Southern British English. Interestingly, Thundy claims that American English and Indian English have a common source from which the common features of American English and Indian English are derived. Accordingly, from examples and observations Indian English can be traced back to the Northern dialects of British English. Therefore, the source of the features as those of Indian English and American English is the Northern British speech. The characteristics of Northern British dialects are found in Indian English :

> Indian English was considerably influenced by the northern dialects of British English such as Irish and Scottish English.

R. C. Goffin suggests that "One may note here how the influence of Scots, and other varieties of English, may be discovered in Indian English . . . " (*Some Notes on Indian English* 25). His analysis shows some affinities between the London (Cockney) dialect and Indian English.

1. The use of /w/ for /v/ was an important characteristic of the vulgar London dialects of the nineteenth century. Indians tend to approximate the /ъ/ with the /a/ of their native languages.
2. The morphemes containing /ø, ð/ in Standard British English show forms with / t, d / in Cockney.
3. In the stressing of /e/ both Cockney and Indian English seem to follow a similar pattern.
4. /z/ has a more limited distribution in both Cockney and Indian English. Words which may have /z/ as a simple coda in Standard British are paralleled by /j/ forms in Cockney and Indian English as in *barrage, camouflage, rouge,* etc.
5. In Cockney and Indian English /ɪ/ and /i/ tend to become /i/ and [i:] finally in unstressed syllables as in *lovely, really, beauty,* etc.

The similarities between Northern dialects and Indian English prove that it is not enough to say that Indian English has the patterns of Southern British English in its language. Thundy concludes that although Indian English is substantially derived from Northern British English with some phonological features of Cockney speech, it is today as in Australia and New Zealand a language of its own with its spoken and literary traditions. The major influence that shaped the linguistic structures and literary genres of Indian English comes from Southern British English, other indigenous Indian languages and the cultural tradition of India. In this context, Mulk Raj Anand observes:

> I hope that my own experiment in writing in the new language, Indian English, along with the works of many other colleagues, will come to be read by Indian students of the English language. This may help to show why Indian English different from the sister languages of our country, as well as from English, is yet an attempted fusion of both. It is a kind of metamorphosis, which is as significant as Irish English or Welsh English or Australian English. (qtd. in Mohan, "Some Aspects" 193).

6. Some Aspects of Style and Language in Earlier Indian English Fiction

To give an idea of the time span it may be mentioned that the first creative work in Indian English fiction, namely Bankim Chandra Chatterjee's *Rajmohan's Wife*, appeared as a serial in the weekly *Indian Field* in 1864, and was published as a book only in 1935. This study however would include in this section a brief analysis of the novels of Mulk Raj Anand, Raja Rao and R. K. Narayan. The features of the language of their novels, which are used consciously, and deliberately for artistic effects and purpose denoted as Indianisms or stylistic devices would be discussed. The process of Indianisation has been noted by several Indian writers as Gokak and Kachru. In this respect, R. K. Narayan makes a significant observation in the following words :

> English has proved that if a language has flexibility, any experience can be communicated through it, even if it has to be paraphrased sometimes rather than conveyed, and even if the factual detail . . . is partially understood . . . . The English language, through . . . resilience and mobility, is . . . undergoing a process of Indianisation, in the same manner as it adopted U. S. citizenship over a century ago, with the difference that it is the major language there, but here one of the fifteen (qtd. in Mohan, "Some Aspects" 193).

An Indian writer in English faced certain problems regarding narrativity, some of which Raja Rao refers to in the preface to *Kanthapura*. He notes: "The telling has not been easy. One has to convey in a language that is not one's own the spirit that is one's own" (5). The characters in the novel *Kanthapura* are village folk. A linguistic analysis of the novel reveals some interesting features of the Kannada element in the novel in the style of story telling, in the descriptions, in the words and in the collocations. The characters of R. K. Narayan's novels are middle class people. The writer has used the method of straightforward translation of Indian expressions in English. The following are translations of some Indian idioms and proverbs from his novels :

> *Bachelor of Arts :* 'To the dust pot with your silly customs.' 'His pen ceased.'
> *The Guide :* 'I left her after food.'; 'How can we think philosophies, not our line, master.'; 'Thin as a broomstick, but talks like a giant' (qtd. in Mohan, "Some Aspects" 197).

Indian English is easily recognisable from Narayan's dialogues. They are readily acceptable to the Indian reader and the non-Indian reader because of the easy flow of Narayan's language. It would be presumptuous to assume that Narayan was unaware of the deviations from native English and it is evident that the anomalous nature of these expressions is not without a reason. Mulk Raj Anand has used devices or Indianisms to create his discourse. These are likely to create some difficulty for the Indian reader who is not conversant with Urdu or Punjabi. Yet it is a remarkable experiment with Indianisms. Indian English like all other languages has become self-generating and its creative use in fiction and other forms of writing today has enriched its resources.

7. English in India

Even though Mulk Raj Anand, Raja Rao, R. K. Narayan and

others in the past and at present illustrate Indian English in their own ways and as a result of interaction of English with other Indian languages, English has affected the phonology and the syntax of the Indian languages and in turn has been influenced by them. The English phonology in India especially, the stops and fricatives are characterised by the stops from the Indian languages. Similarly, Indian English syntax is influenced by the native language syntax in the formation of negatives and questions. There are two aspects to the process that has brought English from the state of being pidgin to the point of being acknowledged as a second language. One aspect is that due to long association with English it ceases to be an alien language. In the course of time it comes to be used in various domains and its use becomes less and less restricted. When a language stays away from its native land for a long time, it begins to take roots in its immediate environment and gets moulded accordingly. Sociolinguists refer to these phenomena as "contextualization."[5] The context not being British, English turned non-British and acquired identities inherent in the immediate contexts.

The other aspect of the process of English becoming a second language is related to the global status of English. English is more than a foreign language in the sense of being restricted to one particular foreign country. English is a world language. This is partly the reason why countries with English as second language have retained English even after attaining political freedom and have granted it the official recognition as a second language. The other reason may be attributed to cultural and linguistic diversity necessitating the use of English as link language. The written mode of Indian English has involved the following aspects:

A. The Print Media and Journalism

> Today Indian English journalism is rated on par with English journalism of other English speaking countries. An indepth historical study of English journalism reveals

the spread of English in India and the process of English acquiring the Indian entity (Sanyal, *Indlish*).

B. Creative and Critical Writing in Indian English

Creative and critical writing in Indian English contributed to the growth of English in India. Indian English literature as a branch of literature has received serious consideration. But the role of Indian English literature in the emergence of Indian English is one aspect, which has not been fully explored. In this context, Sidney Greenbaum states:

> Second-language writers in Southeast Asia . . . are making important contribution to English literature. Their writings may incorporate features characteristic of their second language variety, including rhetorical and stylistic features, but they are generally addressed to, and read by, an international English readership (*A Comprehensive Grammar* 4).

India and the English language have gone through different interactional phases. In the beginning, it was the 'foreigners and natives' type of language contact situations. Indians 'picked up' the English they heard and this 'picked-up' English is seen in use in the earliest writings. In course of time, the language-contact situation broadened and varieties of English—low, middle and high emerged. Moreover, education and the print media helped English broaden its base in India.

Indian English is acquired through formal schooling and the Indian learner's exposure to English. Interference from Indian regional languages occurs at all the three levels: syntactic, lexical and phonological—but particularly at the level of phonology, since it is at this level that the mother tongue influence remains predominant. Because of the virtual absence of contact with native English speech, the Indian learner of

English has no direct exposure to native English phonology. The English spoken by Indians, therefore, shows a remarkable approximation at the level of phonology to the Indian regional languages from which it has absorbed features. The fact that practically all Indians learn English from other Indians has led to the perpetuation of these features. The result is that there are as many forms of spoken English or 'regional accents' as there are language groups in India. These are considered in detail in Chapter III : Phonological Features. The phonological, syntactic and lexical features of English thus acquired in the Indian bilingual context constitute what has come to be known as the Indianness of Indian English, as opposed to the "Englishness" of British English or the "Americanness" of American English. These have generally been viewed as "deviations" from the norms of British English.

Kachru makes a useful distinction between "deviations" and "mistakes" with regard to non-native varieties of English. He remarks :

> A "mistake" may be defined as any "deviation" which is rejected by a native speaker of English as out of the linguistic "code" of the English language, and which may not be justified in Indian English on formal and/or contextual grounds. A "deviation," may involve differences from a norm, but such deviations may be explained in terms of the cultural and/or linguistic context in which a language functions ("The Indianness" 397).

Thus many lexical innovations in Indian English formed as a result of processes such as borrowing, transfer, hybrid formations, literal translations from the L1, idioms, etc., are accepted as appropriate to the Indian social and cultural contexts. As a result of being used in India for a long time, Indian English has developed distinct features in lexical usage. Apart from the use of Indian collocations and the prolific noun compounds, peculiarities in Indian English lexis range from semantic modification of native English words to coinage of new expressions and direct borrowing from the indigenous languages of India.

An inevitable outcome of a bilingual and bicultural situation is the change in the lexicon. It is a sociolinguistic fact that semantic changes can be caused by cultural modifications. As language is unique, societal factors shape specialised meaning among words, among social groups and these new meanings spread throughout the community. In Indian English, new meanings have been added to certain words and existent meanings have been reduced, so that they represent a different semantic range than they do in British English, from which they were originally derived. There is another set of words, which may be termed as of 'typically' Indian English usage. These include lexical items, which are familiar enough to Indian speakers but are not generally known to or rarely used by the majority of native speakers. There are, in addition to these, certain lexical innovations in Indian English, which comprise loan translations and hybrid formations. The latter consist of lexical inventions, which comprise two or more elements, at least one of which is from an Indian language and one from English. These neologisms represent the various aspects of Indian life and culture. Many of these have become fixed collocations in their specific registers. In some cases L1 words and expressions have been taken over into Indian English for lack of exact equivalents in English. These are direct adaptations from the indigenous languages and can be sub-grouped into :

(a) Those which have become part of the lexical stock of the English language and may be termed "assimilated" items following Kachru, since they are used both in British and American English, and
(b) Those items which have not necessarily been included in the lexicon of native varieties of English but have a high frequency in the lexicon of Indian English.

8. Findings

From the review of work done on Indian English, it can be said that scholars have either argued in favour of (Kachru, Verma, Mohan) or against (Narasimhaiah, Nagarajan) accepting Indian English as a variety of English. They have concentrated on certain aspects of Indianness of Indian English at various levels of linguistic analysis—phonology, lexis, syntax and style. Studies of lexical, syntactic and phonological aspects of Indian English will be looked into in the following chapters. An aspect of Indian English is the functional aspect—who speaks English, for what purpose and to whom. The aim of this study is to investigate the domains in which Indian English tends to be used and to highlight linguistic aspects of its form. The following chapter summarises in detail the previous discussions on Indian English.

Notes

1. The link below provides historical documents and information. <http://www.thecore.nus.edu.sg/../../Victorian/authors/macaulay/chron.html> Other documents such as letters exchanged between the Indian Governors-General, East India Company agents and Indian rulers and chiefs, for the period 1759-1795, the originals and associated background materials are in the National Archives of India and the State Archives. Original correspondence E/3, "An Introduction to the Indian Office Library and Records," is found in Oriental and India Office Collections, British Library, London). Richard S. Bingle also documents other such historical sources in an article that appeared in *South Asian Graduate Research Journal* 3 (2) Fall 1996.
2. In a book published in 2005, Kachru notes, "the survey figures . . . add up to 333 million Indians who possess varying degrees of bilingual competence in Indian English" (*Asian Englishes Beyond the Canon* 15).
3. Bilingualism cline ("The Indianness in Indian English," 393-394) is a concept from Kachru, which states that there are three arbitrary measuring points for bilingualism; namely, the zero point, the

central point and the ambilingual point. The zero point is at the bottom point on the axis.

4. L. S. Ramaiah. *Indian English: A Bibliographical Guide to Resources*, New Delhi: Gian Publishing House, 1988.
5. Particularly Kachru mentioned it in *Indianization* 103; *The Alchemy* 12.

Chapter - 2

Review of Literature

This chapter is an account of a review of the literature available on Indian English. Indian English has been widely discussed and brought into focus as a topic of linguistic analysis since the early 1970s. One of the earlier commentators on Indian English, Braj B. Kachru has published his works for forty years from 1965-2005. Publications of some of the other analysts were also contemporaneous and on identical themes. The presentation here is neither chronological nor according to thematic affinity. Hence a number of themes are recurrent in the discussion of the following investigators arranged alphabetically :

1. R. Burchfield
2. C. J. Daswani
3. Braj B. Kachru
4. Yamuna Kachru
5. Bh. Krishnamurthy
6. Rodney F. Moag
7. Ramesh Mohan
8. S. V. Parasher
9. Rani Rubdy
10. Larry E. Smith
11. Kamal K. Sridhar and S. N. Sridhar
12. S. K. Verma

The chapter concludes with respective findings.

1. R. Burchfield

Burchfield in *The Cambridge History of the English Language* notes some of the following grammatical features of educated South Asian English:

Sentence Structure: There is a tendency to use complex over-embedded sentences as opposed to simple sentences in native English. This is for the fact that there are two styles in major South Asian languages, namely, colloquial and formal. The formal style is a 'learned' style and displays excessive lexical ornamentation.

Question Formation: There is a tendency to form information seeking questions without changing the position of the subject and auxiliary items, e.g. *What you would like to eat?, When you would like to go?*

Selectional Restrictions: In English, certain verbs govern certain forms of complements, *want* for example takes only an infinitive complement (*want to read*), *enjoy* only a gerund (*enjoy reading*), and *like* governs both. In South Asian English these restrictions are not adhered to, e.g. from English in South Asia : *The Baluchistan Clerks Association has announced to take out a procession; He doesn't hesitate from using four-letter words.* (*The Cambridge History* 110).

Lexical Resources : South Asian lexical stock borrowed from L1 languages may be divided into three major classes: (1) those which are borrowed from L1 languages as single items and which undergo different types of semantic shift after being borrowed. These are words, single lexical items; (2) those hybrid items, which comprise elements of two or more languages in which one item is from L1. This class involves hybridised lexical items from at least two distinct languages. Hybrid innovations include: hybrid collocations, hybrid lexical sets and hybrid reduplication; (3) those English lexical items, which have undergone semantic extension or restriction in South Asian English. The third class includes English lexical items with deviant semantic connotations and involves several productive processes : (a) Neologisms transferred from underlying South Asian languages, such as *bull work, cousin sister, to break rest.* (b) Innovations formed on the analogy of British English or in some cases American English, for example *caste-proud* formed on the analogy of house-proud. (c) Innovations, which are the result of institutionalisation of English in South Asian socio-cultural contexts for example, ***military hotel*** "a non-vegetarian restaurant."

Investigating the distinctiveness of non-native literatures, Robert Burchfield summarises the following linguistic terms. First, he mentions that creativity entails contextual nativisation of a text. There is a shift from the traditional presuppositions of English, a crossover from one underlying canon to another (Kachru, *Asian Englishes* 91). The nativisation is in the historical and cultural presupposition in the text. Thus English achieves pluricentricity in its cultural presuppositions and in its linguistic norms through such identity. Second, there is an altered concept of textual cohesiveness and cohesion. The organisation of textual structure deviates from the preferred native English structure. It is often a transfer from an underlying dominant language (L1), and may involve a lexical shift: direct lexical transfer or hybridisation or code-switching. Third, the rhetorical strategies differ from the native varieties of English. The rhetorical strategies are similes and metaphors from L1. These result in unusual collocations and combinations for the native speaker. Speech acts and culture-specific interactional markers are translated from South Asian languages.

Lexicalisation : The productive processes used in lexicalisation, according to Burchfield (*The Cambridge History* 537) are: loan words, loan shifts, hybridisation and parallel lexical sets. In loan words there is intrusion of lexical items in every domain (registers of science, technology, fashion, television, cinema and advertising). The parallel lexical sets have roughly the same denotative meaning when transferred in an Indian language. For example, the verb formation in Indian English with the structure V + auxiliary "*wait karna*" is Indianised from the verb 'to wait.' The auxiliary is an additional feature found in Indian languages.

2. C. J. Daswani

C. J. Daswani in his article on "Some Theoretical Implications for Investigating Indian English" mentions Indian English as a variety of English, which shares a specific number of features with Standard English while there are also systematic divergences between Standard English and Indian English.

Daswani states that the learning of L2 is significantly different from the learning of L1 as the L2 learner already controls the grammar of his/her language (L1). The L1 rules may interfere with the learner's acquisition of the L2. As English in India, when L2 (English) is used in communication situations, the linguistic patterns of the L1 and L2 intersect and result in replacement or convergence of linguistic features. The dissimilarity of L1 and L2 learning processes raises certain theoretical implications. When, a bilingual community in a specific domain acquires the L2 variety, the acquired speech variety may differ/deviate from the standard variety (though there can be exceptions). The divergences are found at the phonetic level. According to Daswani, it is possible to identify more than one variety of English of the bilinguals where each variety has a unique set of divergent features from Standard English. In the article investigating Indian English, he examines the deviant usage of nouns and verbs and describes their syntactic and semantic features. He offers no linguistic explanation for the presence or absence of an article before the noun (examples from Dustoor, *The World of Words*); and also for the nouns wrongly inflected for the plural number. As deviant examples of verbs, the transitive-intransitive distinction was absent for many verbs.

In question formations, the movement of the auxiliary to the pre-subject position is considered an Indian English phenomenon. In the written varieties of English, he mentions the use of the following :

1. *would* for *will* (pure futurity)
2. *should* for *ought to* (obligation)
3. past perfect (*had gone*) for simple past (*went*).

According to Daswani, deviations in newspaper English are

idiosyncratic. In other words, not all newspaper English is syntactically deviant. In this context, Mulk Raj Anand conjectures in "Some Notes on Indian English Writing":

> I feel that those who presume to do creative writing in Indian English language are likely to know enough grammar, before they put pen to paper. I tried to analyze very early in my own writing of the English language, the creative process involved. I found, while writing spontaneously, that I was invariably translating dialogue from original Punjabi into English . . . (this) could not have been expressed in any other way except in an almost literal translation, which might carry over the sound (*sic*) and sense of the original speech . . . . This happened usually when I was writing my stories and novels. In the essays, I could control myself and write almost entirely in the English language, as it is written. (239)

The phenomenon of Indian English is a product of a language contact situation. It has resulted from an intricate blending of the semantic-syntactic systems of English and other L1 Indian languages.

3. Braj B. Kachru

In a series of papers and book publications, Braj B. Kachru comments on various aspects of Indian English. In one of his papers, "Indian English: A Sociolinguistic Profile", Kachru denunciates the attitude of linguistic pluralism and pleads for an interrelationship between formal and functional aspects of the English language and later on discusses its functional nativeness (*Asian Englishes* 12). At the pragmatic aspect he makes a strong plea for a new perspective, for a realistic vision and for an understanding toward the third world varieties of English. In his article on "Indian English : A Study in Contextualization", he argues in favour of a "pragmatic" or "functional" view of the uses of non-native varieties of English and Indian English in particular.

At the linguistic level, Kachru's central argument is that "the Indian socio-cultural and linguistic setting has affected features of the English language in India" ("Indian English : A Study" 281). He investigates the Indianness of Indian English, which appears to deviate from native varieties of English. With illustrative material from Indian English literature and journalistic writings, for instance *(I) touch your feet* or *(I) bow my forehead* in an Indian context, he concludes that manifestations in Indian English "are an outcome of the Indianization of English which has, gradually, made Indian English culture-bound in the socio-cultural setting of India" ("The Indianness" 410). He argues that in Indian English there is transfer of Indian cultural patterns to English, transfer of L1 meanings to L2 items, and transfer of form-content components (this point is discussed in Chapter 5).

In *The Alchemy of English*, Kachru introduces the term "alchemy" in the context of functions of English language as "the attitudinal reactions to the status and functions of English across cultures during our times" [1]. In the process, the non-native varieties have brought about changes in the native varieties of English and have resulted in sociolinguistic, linguistic and literary questions being posed about English, which were rarely asked before. He brings the term "non-native" English ("The Indianness") for the transplanted varieties of English, which are acquired primarily as second language. From the 1920s to date, English is the language of political discourse, administration and law. For the Indian government, English serves two purposes. First, it provides a linguistic tool for the administrative cohesion of the country and second, it provides a language of wider communication (national and international). Kachru defines a linguistic innovation as one result of nativisation of English which, in turn is the result of the new ecology in which a non-native variety of English functions. Indian English has been through this process since the seventeenth century. Nativisation of English includes lexical and collocational changes, stylistic innovations (e.g., code-mixing), functional varieties, reactions to the development of non-native English literatures and to thematic and stylistic nativisation and innovations displayed in such texts. Commenting on nativisation of the language, by South Asian novelists, Kachru remarks:

> South Asian novelists not only nativized the language by extensive stylistic experimentation, but also acculturated English in terms of South Asian context. The processes of nativization vary in their subtlety from one writer to another (*Asian Englishes* 58).

According to Kachru, English in India has four major functions. They are instrumental, regulative, interpersonal, and innovative (or creative). English has instrumental function, as it is the medium of learning at various stages. As the language of the legal system and pan-Indian administration, English performs a regulative function. An important role of English is that it provides a code of communication to linguistically and culturally diverse groups for interpersonal communication. This role symbolises elitism, prestige and modernity. The use of English has resulted in the development of a significant body of South Asian English writing. This is its innovative function. In his description of Phonetics and Phonology, Kachru talks about series substitution, systemic differences, distributional differences and prosodic differences of Indian English. Series substitution involves the substitution of retroflex consonants for the alveolar series: e.g. [T] and [D] substituted for English [t] and [d]. Systemic differences are related to syllables. In Indian languages and as it is in English, consonant-vowel-consonant (CVC) morpheme structure is possible. South Asian languages, particularly Indian languages, do not use [f], [ø] or [ð] and do not distinguish between the "dark" and "clear" varieties of [l]. The sounds [f], [ø] and [ð] are generally realised as [ph], [th] and [d] or [dh] respectively. Distributional differences entail a type of transfer. The consonant clusters *sk, sl* and *sp*, etc., even though found in Indian languages do not occur word initially or as the initial phoneme of a word. Therefore, there is a difference in pronunciation; for instance, in the lexical items: [iskul] school, [isteʃan] station, and so on. Indian English is prosodically different as it is syllable-timed like most Indian languages whereas native English variety is stress-timed.

In the grammar section, Kachru discusses about the use of complex sentences and large-scale embedding, interrogative sentences and the formation of tag questions, the use of stative predicates (is having, seeing, knowing), and the use of the articles as "missing," "intrusive," "wrong," "usurping," and "disposed". He describes reduplication as a feature of non-native variety, which is used for emphasis and to indicate continuation of a process. He notes: "For Raja Rao, reduplication of a phrase provides the effect of colloquial speech, as well as giving linguistic clues to mark a character type" (*Indianization* 79).. For collocational structures, a native speaker of English might use a clause or a nominal group whereas a non-native speaker prefers modifier + head + (qualifier) structure. For example, *welcome address* as opposed to *an address of welcome*.

Kachru mentions code mixing as a characteristic feature of non-native English. The motivations for code mixing with English are role identification; register identification, elucidation, status indication and elitism. Taking the bilingual competence of the readers for granted, code mixing from South Asian languages with English is found in newspapers. Kachru cites the following example : "Pan masalà causes rare disease" (*Asian Englishes* 114).

There are three roles of English, according to Kachru, in a non-native English user's linguistic repertoire. First, the range of Englishes can vary from pidgin English to "Standard" English. Second, different varieties are used in different roles of intra-national and international functions. Third, there is a relationship between the variety and the participant in a linguistic interaction. This, he mentions, is an attempt toward the contextualisation of Englishes within a context of situation. He mentions several reasons as to why the non-native varieties deviate at the phonological, grammatical, and lexical levels. These are (i) the presence of a substratum, (ii) the impact of cultural parameters, (iii) resistance to the impact of linguistic changes which influences the native varieties of English, and (iv) primary importance to written sources, especially those of the eighteenth and nineteenth centuries. This is labelled as "bookishness" in Indian English (*Indianization* 41).

According to Kachru there are parameters of appropriateness, which determine the deviations of Indian English. The deviations are register-restricted and genre-restricted. A large number of deviations also result from the process of acculturation, which makes the non-native varieties of English culture-bound, and creates distances between other varieties.

English in India is a transplanted language, at the same time, an acquired language, which is learnt after the speakers have learnt their mother tongue. A language may be considered transplanted if it is used by a significant number of speakers in social, cultural, and geographical contexts different from the contexts in which it was originally used. A transplanted language functions in new surroundings, in new roles and in new contexts. The salient characteristics of the creativity of the bilingual are :

(a) the process used in creativity is based on multi-norms of styles and strategies;
(b) nativisation and acculturation of text presupposes an altered context of situation for the language. Traditionally accepted literary norms with reference to a particular code (e.g., Hindi or English) do not operate here;
(c) the creativity of the bilinguals results in the configuration of two or more codes. The resultant code contextualises in terms of the new uses of languages, and
(d) such creativity is not merely a formal combination of two or more underlying language designs, but a creation of cultural, aesthetic, societal, and literary norms. The creativity has a distinct context of situation.

Authenticity (Indianness) to the speech acts is achieved by linguistic realisation of the following types: (1) the use of native similes and metaphors, (2) the transfer of rhetorical devices for "personalising" speech interaction, (3) the translation ("transcreation") of proverbs and idioms, (4) the use of culturally-dependent speech styles, and (5) the use of syntactic devices.

The English language has been South Asianised, and became a part of the culture. The process of South Asianisation, particularly, Indianisation of the English language, is manifested in different aspects. It supplies rich data for language contact study in a cross-cultural and multilinguistic context and raises theoretical and methodological problems about the descriptions of the new Englishes, which have developed from the native varieties of English. The linguistic study of the features of the deviant variety in relation to typically Indian context are:

1. Register Variation
2. Style Variation
3. Collocational Deviation
4. Semantic Shifts
5. Lexical Change.

1. Register Variation

The term register means a restricted language, which is contextually delimited on the basis of formal features. A register in South Asia (particularly India), both contextually and formally, has certain features, which are absent in the native varieties of English (Kachru, "Indian English: A Study" 268). A number of register determined terms are found in the newspapers published in English in India and in other Indian writing.

2. Style Variation

The term style broadly means the sense in which it is used in literature. "It refers to those formal features of a text which enable us to distinguish not only the participants but also the *situational determined choices* which are made by a writer out of the total closed-system or open-set choices possible in a language" (*English in South Asia* xv). An example of extremely Indianised use of style variation is found in Raja Rao's *Kanthapura*. The following examples of nominal groups that occur in the novel are formally deviants from the native varieties of English: *cardamom-field Ramchandra* (19); *corner-house Moorthy* (5); *four-beamed house Chandrasekharayya* (22); *front-house Akkamma* (4); *gap-tooth Siddayya* (10); *iron-shop Imam Khan* (133); and *that-house people* (21).

Commenting on the stylistic innovations that flowered in Raja Rao, Mulk Raj Anand and others Kachru notes ". . . in current creative writing (e.g., of Salman Rushdie, . . . Amitav Ghosh, Vikram Seth . . .) such creativity has become almost a marker of "liberation" in Indian English Writing" ("South Asian English" 17).

3. Collocational Deviations

These may be due to grammatical deviations from the varieties of English which are used as the first language or, there may be loan shifts or lexis-bound translations from Indian languages (Kachru, "The Indianness," "Indian English: A study"); or the deviation may be contextual and not formal. This may result in a semantic shift of an English lexical item.

4. Semantic Shifts

An item of English has additional semantic markers in deviant varieties; which are not assigned in the native varieties of English, e.g. *government* or *master* as modes of address. These lexical items are redefined in terms of Indian contextual units. The semantic features of Indian English may be characterised as semantic restriction of English words, semantic extension of

English words, archaisms preserved in Indian English and not current in native English variety, and contextual redefinition of lexical items.

5. Lexical Change

A number of Indianisms are found in the verb syntax, as mentioned by A. F. Kindersley. In the examples the verb *to do* (transitive) or *to run* or *to come* (intransitive), are discussed.

(a) *I am doing* for *I* (*constantly*) *do*. Similarly *I was doing* for *I* (*constantly*) *did*.
(b) *I am doing it* (for *I have been doing it*) *since six months*.
(c) *I did* for *I have* (*just or hitherto*) *done*.
(d) *I had run* for *I ran*.
(e) *It is done* for *It has been done*; and *It was done* for *It had been done*.
(f) *If I did* for *If I do*.
(g) *When I will come* and *If I will come* for *When I come* and *If I come*.
(h) *May* in jussive sense. cf. *You may kindly come, I may* (for *let me*) *go*.
(i) *This may be done* for *Please do this*.
(j) *For doing* for *to do*.
(k) Idiomatic use of the perfect participle active (qtd. in Kachru, *Indianization* 34-35).

Grammatical characteristics mark 'educated' Indian English as deviant from the 'educated' native varieties of English. The sentence and clause structure of Indian English has some deviant features. For example, there is a tendency toward using complex noun and verb phrases and long sentences. The following is an excerpt from *Kanthapura*: "The day rose into the air and with it rose the dust of the morning, and the carts began to creak round the bulging rocks and the coppery peaks, and the sun fell into the river and pierced it to the pebbles, while the carts rolled on and on, fair carts of the Kanthapura fair. . . " (55). There are distinctive features in the constructions at the phrase level (verb phrase or noun phrase). For example, the, be + verb + ing constructions in Indian English. In the formation of interrogative constructions Indian English speakers do not change the position of the subject and the auxiliary items. The tag questions in Indian English show the influence of the first languages. It is not uncommon to find a general 'it' or a negative particle in the tag question: e.g., *You have taken the book, isn't it ? He has borrowed the book, no?* These deviant syntactic varieties according to Kachru, are assimilated items in Indian English.

English as a non-native language is divided into two broad categories, namely, the performance varieties and the institutional varieties. Institutional varieties have some ontological status and they include those varieties, which are used as second languages. At the pragmatic level, Kachru suggests two models in describing the special characteristics of the English speech community. According to the mono-model approach, there is a homogeneous English L2 speech community where the functional roles assigned to English in each are more or less identical. The goals for the study of English in different regions of the world are more or less similar. A poly-model approach is based upon pragmatism and functional realism. It presupposes that there are three types of variability in teaching English for cross-cultural communications; namely, variability related to acquisition, variability related to function and variability related to the contact of situation.

In a retrospective look at English's diaspora varieties, particularly Indian English, Kachru specifically relates some concerns. The first concern relates to a variety of a language and its identity. The term *identity* is used in a regional sense and recognises the uses and the users of a variety as members of an identifiable speech fellowship. The issues of identity also relate other complex sets of interrelated issues such as the attitude toward a variety and its users and the perception of its social and functional usefulness. The second concern is about attitudes toward acculturation of a variety. According to him there is a variable, which determines the attitudes toward acculturation of a variety and acceptance of such acculturation. The functional sense recognises 'Indian' contexts and domains of use as sociolinguistically and functionally appropriate for acculturation of language. For the non-native diaspora varieties of English, he considers the perspectives of the native users of English in the inner circle (primarily English as mother tongue) and the non-native users from the outer circle (ESL). The third concern is to recapitulate various approaches used in the description and analysis of Indianness in English.

4. Yamuna Kachru

Yamuna Kachru in "Linguistics and Written Discourse in Particular Languages" accounts for the discourse properties of Indian English in terms of shared cultural knowledge of the users of the variety. She mentions that in the context of acquisition of English, the primary language acquisition environment determines the background knowledge of the non-native learner for language processing. This knowledge she says, includes both tacit and conscious knowledge along with linguistic and contextual knowledge. This English is consequently nativised with native characteristic features in spoken and written forms. In "Discourse Analysis, Non-Native Englishes" she notes this background knowledge as norms of communicative competence (223). In another article on "Culture, Style and Discourse: Expanding Noetics of English" she defines the notion "noetics" as the role of language in shaping, storage, retrieval and communication of knowledge.

5. Bh. Krishnamurthy

Bh. Krishnamurthy comments on the existence of Indian English as an independent variety of English language. Krishnamurthy observes the following phonetic variations:

English	*Indian*
[f]	[ph] (Gujarati, Marathi)
[w,v]	[b] (Oriya, Bengali, Assamese)
[w,v]	[w/v] (Dravidian languages)
[s, s]	[s] (Oriya, Assamese)
	[s] (Bengali)

English pronunciation in India has regional varieties due to

(a) dominant mother tongue phonology, and
(b) the spelling of written English.

This according to him, could have been avoided if the spellings were reformed or regularised in the teaching of English as a second language. Also, in Indian English pronunciation, stress is totally absent or it sometimes occurs without concomitant vowel changes. After a long vowel, double consonant in spelling is pronounced single because of a phonological rule in length alteration in Indian languages :

$$C / V— \approx C C / V— \#$$

Initial voiceless stops are not aspirated which, according to Bansal (*Intelligibility of Indian English* 159) results in unintelligibility of Indian English to native speakers.

6. Rodney F. Moag

Rodney F. Moag has worked in the field of World Englishes and dealt with the complexities concerning how English functions around the world. In his article on "The Life Cycle of Non-Native Englishes : A Case Study" he states : "...indigenisation is a process of language change by which the new variety of English becomes distinct from the parent imported variety, and from other indigenized varieties elsewhere" (235). In the initial phase of indigenisation process, according to him, there are conditions where the local learners of English are exposed to native speaker models while they use English for communication. In such conditions, there is a probability of reinforcement of native-like features in the language; for which there is no equivalent in the imported native-speaker model of English. In the second phase of indigenisation process, English is used as a lingua franca in addition to the local link languages. In this phase there is transfer of more native features in English. These include additional lexemes and grammatical features through direct transfer or overgeneralisation. The second-language issues mentioned by Ramchand are topical here: ". . . difficulties of expression arising from an inadequate grasp of basic features of the language" and "an author who thinks in one language instinctively and writes in another is liable to modify the adopted language" (*The West Indian Novel* 78).

7. Ramesh Mohan

Ramesh Mohan in his study on some aspects of style and language in Indian English fiction regards Indian English works of fiction as a convincing rendering of the speech of non-English speaking characters in non-English situations. In most novels, transliteration of Indian words and phrases in English script co-exist with literal translations. He distinguishes conscious and deliberate uses of Indianisms and stylistic devices in the works of Mulk Raj Anand, Raja Rao, R. K. Narayan and Kamala Markandaya. According to him, most Indian writers in English mark it as a distinct variety in idiom, imagery and collocational deviations. Also it is necessary to distinguish Indian English from other varieties of English because: ". . . a purely descriptive linguistic analysis of Indian English fiction may create the impression that even such stylistic and linguistic devices as have sometimes been used by novelists to render the speech of non-English speaking characters are features of the variety of English termed as Indian English" (Mohan, "Some Aspects" 192).

8. S. V. Parasher

S. V. Parasher in his *Indian English Functions and Form* mentions varieties in language, particularly those non-native varieties of English which are homogeneous and whose large repertoire of elements function in all contexts of communication. According to him, English, in India has co-existed with several Indian languages and was thus 'X-ized'[1] or 'nativized'. It did not however become the mother tongue of the local English using community, but several non-native varieties of English came into existence. In the theoretical approach to the study of bilingualism, he discusses sociological and sociolinguistic approaches to bilingualism and the spread of English bilingualism in India.

Of the ten sections that the work contains, the first section is about varieties of language, where native and non-native varieties of English have been differentiated. In the second section, bilingualism and language use, the meaning of bilingualism, its description, psychological study of bilingualism, linguistic study of bilingualism, domains of language use, speech community and verbal repertoire, diglossia, triglossia, and polyglossia are discussed. In the following section, Parasher notes the spread of English in higher education, print media, electronic media, administration, social circles, and creative writing. Apart from English bilingualism in India, Parasher, in the fourth section, considers Indian English in Indo-socio-cultural context, Englishness of Indian English, educated Indian English, different registers of Indian English, and linguistic descriptions (phonetics and phonology, lexis, style, syntax, etc.). According to him, studies on Indian English syntax have isolated syntactic 'mistakes,' 'deviations,' 'irregularities' (for example, Kachru "The Indianness," Verma "Code-switching") which can be categorised as "excessive use of complex sentence, use of certain non-progressive verbs in the progressive form (Bandyopadhyay, "Present Continuous in Anurag Mathur's *The Inscrutable Americans*"), erratic use of the article system, . . . and so on" (Parasher, *Indian English* 60). In the fifth section, there is a survey on the use of English in the context of who speaks English, for what purpose, to whom and to what end. The sixth section is about a pattern in the use of languages, especially, for the bilinguals. The mother tongue or the first language is dominant language in the domain of family, and English dominates the areas of education, government and employment. Parasher discusses five domains, namely, the domains of government, education, transactions, neighbourhood, and friendship and concludes that for each of these domains, English is used more in written communication than in face-to-face interaction.

The seventh section investigates the variables that determine the language choice of educated Indian bilinguals, that is, the use of English *vis-à-vis* the mother tongue. The findings show that English is associated with formality and the mother tongue with informality and intimacy. Further, the bilinguals tend to use more English when they move out of their linguistic regions. Educated bilinguals use more English and there is a correlation between high status jobs and the use of English. Based on a pilot study on subjects with different educational backgrounds, the author concludes that reading habit also determines the individual's preference for a language. The eighth section is about language attitudes such as language preference and language use and the ninth section is on a survey of English usage in which he aims at showing the differences and similarities between non-native and native varieties of English. He concludes the tenth section with a discussion on Indian English-style, its functions and form.

In a strongly worded paper, "Indian English: Certain Grammatical, Lexical and Stylistic Features," Parasher points out that Indian English, being a non-native language for most Indian bilinguals, has certain characteristics of its own. The educated variety of Indian English, he states, should conform to major syntactic rules of British English, and as a non-native-Indian-variety, show certain differences at the lexical and stylistic levels. In this context, he describes some of the major unacceptable forms beginning with syntax, lexis, and style. The following, according to Parasher, are some of the deviations :

Nominals: In the native variety of English, whenever there is a choice between nominal compounds of the structure N + Prep + N and N + N; native speakers tend to prefer the latter.

Determiners and Modifiers: The deviant forms in this category are articles. The accepted native usage of article seldom hinders communication. Unacceptable forms in the use of other determiners and modifiers relate to the difference between *few* and *a few*, *some* and *a few, much* and *very*.

Word Order: Most Indian languages are of Subject Object Verb (SOV) type unlike English, which is of Subject Verb Object (SVO) type. The deviant forms were related to the position of adverbs, post-posed adjectives and embedded questions. Under this category, Parasher cites the following examples :

1. The heavy lab work I have *now here* (here now)
2. I *will be definitely* joining (will definitely be)
3. Cosmic ray methods *also should be* tried (should also be)

Since adverbs and adverbials are relatively flexible in English, the non-native expressions sometimes deviate from the native expressions.

Verb Patterns : The major sources of deviations to the native speaker are the use of some transitive verbs intransitively, such as, *avail*, *inform*, *assure*, and *request*. Another deviation between native and non-native English (Indian English) is a pattern as *may + infinitive* and *may + be + infinitive* in *that* clauses following the verbs *suggest* and *recommend*, where the native speaker preferred the subjunctive with the base form of the verb. It is to be noted here that :

> The subjunctive is not an important category in contemporary English and is normally replaced by other constructions . . . . The use of the subjunctive occurs chiefly in formal styles (and especially in AmE) where in less formal styles one would make use of other stylistic devices such as *to infinitive* or *should + infinitive* (Quirk *et al.*, *A Grammar of Contemporary English* 76).

The phrase *with a view* is generally followed by the *–ing* form of the verb in native varieties, whereas in Indian English both, the infinitive and *–ing* forms are noticed.

Auxiliaries: The deviants relate to the use of modals. The non-native speakers prefer *would* while the native speakers use *will*. In expressions like *I would not be able to revise the draft*, *I hope you would appreciate the circumstances*, *would* is replaced by *will*. Similarly, the natives prefer *could* to *can*. The use of the modal verbs varied because modality is a semantic notion and the use of an appropriate modal verb depends on the exact meaning the speaker/writer wishes to convey.

Tense and Aspect: The use of present perfect for the simple past is a feature of the non-native variety. This usage is acceptable in the native variety (Trudgill, *Sociolinguistic Patterns* 13). According to Hughes and Trudgill this usage is an "ongoing grammatical development" which may be "the beginning of a change in the language" (*English Accents* 9). In Parasher's observation, Verma quotes several examples of this usage from formal documents produced in India and native English-speaking countries and suggests that it may be the "result of interaction between the native and non-native varieties of English" ("Indian English" 32). A similar instance was observed for the past tense. Indian English speakers prefer the past progressive use where the native speakers prefer simple past. For example, the construction, *the method we were using sometime ago*. A tendency in Indian English is the present progressive use where the native varieties prefer perfective aspect of the present progressive, as in *I am running a boutique for the past four years*.

Prepositions: There are three tendencies in Indian English with respect to the use of prepositions: (i) to delete, (ii) to add, and (iii) to use inappropriately certain prepositions. The non-native user has little motivation to conform to the native standard as the above mentioned tendencies rarely distort the message to be communicated.

Parasher also discusses clause connectors and clause structure, S-V concord and constituent structure and category structure. In "lexis," the deviant sources are: (i) redundant lexical items, (ii) neologisms, and (iii) stylistically inappropriate items. Here are some examples which are features of Indian English with the native acceptable forms within brackets:

1. we were *directed to* (asked/told to)
2. kindly do the *needful* [what (ever) is necessary]
3. *at an early date* (as soon as possible)
4. it is *highly imperative* (necessary)
5. we shall be *highly obliged* [(most) grateful]
6. I shall be *thankful* (grateful) if you . . .

Indian English speakers tend to use formal lexical items and native speakers prefer an informal or less formal lexical item.

7. the work on this project is yet to *commence* (start/begin)
8. *extend* (give us) your cooperation

Some deviations in collocations are:

9. We *invite your attention* (draw your attention) to
10. Kindly *enhance* (increase) our overdraft limit...

In native varieties *invite* does not collocate with *attention* and *enhance* collocates with words relating to quality rather than quantity. Under "style," stylistically appropriate and acceptable forms from the corpus are discussed. The non-native speakers prefer nominal forms whereas the natives prefer verbal forms:

1. This has *reference* (refers) to your letter
2. Please acknowledge *the receipt of* (receiving) this letter

Indians and the native speakers of English express the notion of English differently. In the native variety, polite request is usually expressed by past form of modals or with a conditional construction: *will/would* in the *if*-clause as well as the main clause. In the non-native varieties, with *will/would/could* in the *if*-clause only. A feature of Indian English is extremely polite style. The following are some such instances :

1. *Kindly* please advise me

2. I wish to bring to your *kind* notice
3. I *invite* your *kind* attention
4. I *respectfully submit* the following few lines *for favour* of your *kind* consideration
5. your *esteemed* help
6. With due respect I beg to inform you
7. *I have the honour to invite* a reference to your letter
8. I *request your honour*

The choice of address forms in Indian English is wider than native varieties of English; such as *respected sir*, *yours respectfully/respectfully yours*, etc. These are unacceptable to the native speaker. The deviant lexical forms and stylistic usages are characteristic features of Indian English. The choice of style largely depends on interpersonal relationship between the addresser and the addressee in particular socio-cultural settings. And this is a difference in style between the native speakers and Indian English users. Educated Indian English thus has marked differences in lexis and style as compared with native educated varieties.

9. Rani Rubdy

Rani Rubdy in her dissertation on "A Study of Some Written Varieties of Indian English" classifies the features of Indian English under the areas of syntax, lexico-semantics and cohesion. She studies the deviations from a sample of educated Indian English speakers in India along the cline of Indian English bilingualism. The following are the deviations noted by Rubdy:

Articles

For the Indian English speakers of English the articles are difficult due to the absence of a parallel category in the deictic system of most Indian languages. Deviations arise from the speaker's failure to observe certain restrictions on article usage. For instance, uncountables and plurals do not take articles unless when specified with reference to something. Similarly proper nouns have 'unique' reference in the context and, therefore, do not normally take an article in English. The common deviant usages of articles in Indian English, classified according to their possible causes are :

1. Intrusion of the definite article with proper nouns (e.g., *The* Victoria lake).
2. The intrusion of the definite article with uncountables and plurals in their non-specific use (e.g., . . . promotion of *the* studies).
3. Nominalisation of expressions as the noun normally collocates with an article. (e.g., down to *the* earth, last but not *the* least, *the* ways and means).
4. The intrusion of an indefinite article with uncountables (e.g., It is *a* year round work).
5. The omission of the definite article in its 'particularising' function. Indian English is often characterised by the absence of the definite article where it is obligatory in native English to denote specificity (e.g., . . . as makers and moulders of ø[2] younger generation).
6. The omission of the definite article in contexts where idiomatic usage requires it (e.g., A bridge across ø Godavari. . .).
7. Omission of the definite article where it is normally used to emphasise the uniqueness of the persons or things referred to. Since the objects are unique, for an Indian English speaker, they appear to need no specification (e.g., . . . ø planet earth, . . . the role which ø English language plays).
8. Omission of the indefinite article in contexts that denote specificity (e.g., . . . such ø state of affairs).
9. The use of the definite article instead of the indefinite and vice versa.

Prepositions

Deviant use of prepositions is found in Indian English for the fact that there are no prepositions in quite a few Indian languages.

Instead, Indian languages are characterised by the occurrence of postpositions which perform somewhat similar functions as prepositions do in English. For the L2 speaker there is a temptation to assume that a set of words that are related in meaning may collocate with the same preposition. A part of deviant usage is due to this assumption. As to whether a particular word requires a preposition as a collocation or not is another source of deviant usage. Indian English users show a tendency to add prepositions after verbs. English verbs optionally collocate with prepositions. There are also instances where Indian English users omit prepositions where native speakers would consider them indispensable. In words which have common morphemic representations as nouns and verbs, the language allows only the nouns to be combined with prepositions; the verbs generally do not take prepositions after them. Indian English speakers tend to use prepositions with the corresponding verbs.

Tense

The mother tongue or L1 influence on Indian English tense is conspicuous. In many Indian languages, tense is not as rigid as it is in English. English has several rules regarding inter-clause and inter-sentential tense concord. In Indian languages tense is more flexible. In Indian English, according to Rubdy ("A Study" 199), deviations in tense are of the following forms :

1. Violation of sequence of tenses,
2. Use of the Past Perfect and the Present Perfect for the Simple Past,
3. Use of the Past Perfect for the Present Perfect,
4. Use of Simple Present for the Present Perfect Progressive, and
5. Use of the progressive with verbs of perception and state.

Indian English speakers as in Indian languages, use the

simple Past and the Past Perfect as free variants. In certain situations in English, where simple past would be used, Indian languages require Past Perfect to refer to a completed action which took place at a certain time in the past (e.g., I went there last week). There is not always a one-to-one correspondence between the Past Perfect and the simple Past in English and their counterparts in Indian languages, and this difference is carried over in the English of L2 speakers of English.

The use of Past Perfect in Indian English where native speakers of English prefer the Present Perfect is due to the emphasis on the completion of the activity in the past rather than its relevance to the present. Furthermore, Indian English speakers deviate in the use of the Present Perfect Progressive as the Indian tense system does not have the progressive aspect of the Present Perfect and it is substituted by the simple Present. In the Indian tense system, an act of continuing at the time of speaking, even if it began at a certain time in the past, belongs to the present. Therefore, this is assumed as Present Progressive by Indian English speakers. Verbs of perception and state except those with a change of meaning are rarely used in the progressive tense in English. Native speakers learn the distinction between the verbs of state (such as *like, want, own, belong*, etc.) process through early exposure to language. For foreign speakers this distinction is not always clear as these are also found in the progressive with special meanings.

Modals

Deviant usage in Indian English with regard to modals, as Rubdy ("A Study" 211) mentions, comprises the indiscriminate use of 'will' and 'would,' and the substitution of 'may' where native speakers would have used 'should' or 'ought to' or 'must.' In native English, 'will' is used when talking of the 'pure future,' i.e., when future events are not influenced by willingness, intention or likelihood or any external circumstances. 'Going to' or 'likely to' is preferred when the latter are considered. Indian

English speakers are usually unaware of this distinction, and use 'will' instead.

Word Order

English has a fixed word order and changes in the sequence of words lead to changes in meaning such as those in terms of contrast, emphasis, etc. Indian English speakers, at the upper end of the bilingualism cline show little deviation in this area in spite of the striking difference between the SVO word order of English and the SOV order of most Indian languages. Indian English speakers show deviations in their use of the adverbials. Adverbs of frequency occur at mid-position while adverbs of time at the beginning or end of a sentence. An adverb of place or direction follows the verb with which it is semantically related. Other adverbs and adverb phrases take end positions. These positions are not fixed and change of place stands for emphasis. These complexities are likely to confuse the L2 speaker.

Deviation in word order is found in pre-posing of adjectives from their positions as post-head modifiers in certain expressions. Indian English speakers tend to normalise such phrases as initiated below in b (1) and c (1) where the post-head modifier is pre-posed to a pre-nominal position on the analogy of the constructions as in a (2).

a (1) The categories mentioned above
a (2) The above mentioned categories
b (1) *the authorities concerned*
b (2) the concerned authorities
c (1) *the persons responsible*
c (2) the responsible persons

Non-Count Nouns Used as Count Nouns

English nouns fall into two broad categories of count and non-count nouns. The members of the two categories behave differently in language. Non-count nouns do not occur with the indefinite article and they are not pluralised with '–s'. Some of these are treated as count nouns by Indian English speakers, that is, they are used with plural morpheme '–s' and with the indefinite article. This is because the distinction does not exist in Indian languages and due to the complexity of the subject. This complexity is summed up by Jespersen as follows :

> The distinction between thing-words (countables) and mass-words (uncountables) is easy enough if we look at the idea that is expressed in each single instance. But in practical language the distinction is not carried through in such a way that one and the same word stands always for one and the same idea. On the contrary, a great many words in one connection stand for something countable and in another for something uncountable (*Essentials of English Grammar* 206-207).

In some Indian languages, the nouns corresponding to information such as news work are count nouns. But they are non-count in English. Many nouns can be either count or non-count (with some differences in meaning). Quirk *et al.*, (*A Comprehensive Grammar* 251-252) give the following examples:

> He didn't give much *information*, and
> A *piece*/*bit*/*word* of information.
> Expensive *furniture* and
> A *piece*/an *article*/a *suit* of furniture.

The deviant usages of the L2 speaker of English are due to these variations. Having seen a noun as a countable in one context they assume that it will be countable in another. A study on the nature of the deviant usages in Indian English shows the following instances :

1. The noun in question has both countable and uncountable functions depending upon the meaning which is intended (e.g., *invitation, opinion, work*).

2. The noun is semantically related to other nouns, which are countable (e.g., work: *jobs*, vacation: *holidays*, equipment: *tools*).
3. The noun in question is an uncountable one modified by a unit noun in native English, whereas Indian English speakers modify the noun with the plural morpheme suffix (e.g., *furnitures* for *pieces of furniture*).
4. The noun occurs as an uncountable noun in certain fixed expressions but in Indian English is used in the plural (e.g., climate of *opinions*, acts of *omissions* and *commissions*).
5. Indian English speakers tend to use the noun as a count noun as it has a countable counterpart in Indian languages (e.g., fruits).
6. The noun is never used as a count noun in native English but is pluralised in Indian English (e.g., *tuitions, clarifications, educations, ruminations*).

Pluralisation of a noun can be [+ count] but not [– count]. Nouns with more than one meaning are categorised as countable or uncountable according to the intended meaning. In Indian English, they are sometimes treated as count nouns when the intended meaning is their use as non-count nouns: e.g., Inter-regional cultural activities and *group travels* are organised.

Gerund and the 'to' Infinitive

In Indian English, the functions of the gerund and the 'to' infinitive are often overlapped. In the deviant forms there is discriminate substitution of one for the other. Probably this may be due to the fact that a near-synonym of the verbs before the infinitive construction may be followed by either the gerund or the infinitive without any drastic change of meaning. With certain verbs, the 'to' infinitive is not interchangeable with the '–ing' form. This variation is responsible for a majority of deviant usage in Indian English. Rubdy ("A Study" 237) mentions that

Indian users of English have a tendency to use the infinitive instead of the '–ing' form with the phrase 'with a view to'; e.g., . . . collect the information *with a view to complete* a concise history of the city. In native English, this phrase is followed by the gerund form of the verb. Indian English users prefer to use 'for –ing' to express purpose in contexts where the native speakers use the 'to' infinitive (e.g. *for conducting, for providing, for regaining*). In native English, 'for –ing' describes the use of things and the verb with 'to' is used as an adjunct of purpose. Variations are found because the verb stem with 'to' as an adjunct of purpose has a completing construction in the shape of 'for –ing'. Thus the constructions: 'a box to keep things' and 'a box for keeping things,' both are in use.

Transitive/Intransitive Verbs

The L2 speaker of English is in general unfamiliar with the range of contexts in which particular verbs can be used transitively or intransitively. This results in inappropriate use of these verbs. In the following examples, transitive verbs in the constructions are without direct objects in the context, a norm considered obligatory by native speakers :

1. Mary Barker further *substantiates* in processing.
2. The readers who know more about this kindly *intimate* whether these stamps have been used.

Conversely, some Indian English speakers prefer direct object with intransitive verbs in contexts where they normally do not occur in native English.

Reflexive/Non-Reflexive Verbs

Sometimes Indian English speakers omit the reflexive pronoun in contexts where in native usage it is considered obligatory. And they also tend to prefer the reflexive pronoun where it is not necessary. Many Indian languages do not have a one to one correspondence with the English reflexive. In most Dravidian languages the reflexive pronoun is realised in the third person only. In English, there is a parallel system of personal pronouns corresponding to those used with the reflexive verbs (such as *avail himself*, *settle themselves*, etc.).

Modification

According to Rubdy, as far as modifications are concerned, "IE [Indian English] speakers tend to deviate primarily in the use of degree expressions, more specifically in the use of adverbs such as *quite* and *very* and *much* and the use of intensifiers with adjectives that are normally considered 'absolute' such as *perfect, unique* etc." ("A Study" 254). *Quite*, as an adverb, has two meanings. One meaning is completely; wholly; absolutely. The other meaning is fairly; reasonably; sufficiently. Also, the use of *quite* as a pre-modifier where the native speaker prefers *very* is traceable to the partial overlapping of meaning and function that exists between these two words. Some Indian English speakers use both very and much together, treating their combination as a compound modifier. The use of degree expressions (perfect, unique, etc.) is considered slovenly and 'bad English' even among native speakers, who tend to do this in everyday speech (258). Indian English speakers prefer degree expressions to modify adjectives as they do not distinguish between 'absolute' adjectives that do not take modifiers and 'ordinary adjectives', which do. To quote some examples :

1. The election is *much more crucial* because it is the forerunner to the assembly elections.
2. . . . without caring to understand the *very essential* and valuable services rendered by them.

N + N Type Construction

In Indian English, nominal groups of a substantive + a

substantive combination are common. The N + N type constructions serve to compress underlying propositions into shorter configurations. Thus they form compact expressions without loss of essential meaning. The following are the processes by which they are derived from underlying propositions:

1. Pre-posing of post head modifier :

   (a) interest rate
   (b) traffic rules
   (c) roadside stall

2. Compression of entire clause into nominal groups by the process of simplification. All other elements are deleted :

   (a) minor child (a child who is a minor)
   (b) loan amounts (amounts given as loan)
   (c) leave travel concession (concession granted while travelling on leave).

3. Nominal groups which are constructed on the analogy of other groups/noun compounds which are common in the language :

   (a) day train ⟶ from night train
   (b) salary limit ⟶ from speed limit
   (c) road hazard ⟶ from occupational hazard

4. –ing forms as pre-nominal modifiers:

   (a) shifting families
   (b) time-barring assessments

5. Hybrid formations in which one element is borrowed from L1 :

(a) Formation in which the head word is a borrowed element :
   (i) cycle rickshaw, (ii) truck wallah.
(b) Formation in which the pre-head modifier is a borrowed element :
   (i) paan shop, (ii) bazaar repairers.

6. Nominal groups in which English lexical items are collocated to denote meanings peculiarly Indian :

   (a) circuit house
   (b) dearness allowance.

Lexical Deviations

In Indian English, contextual differences from the native variety have added new lexical items in the language and given them extended semantic markers. Besides typically Indian collocations and nominal compounds, Indian English lexicon variety consists of semantic modification of native English words, coinage of new expressions and direct borrowing from the indigenous Indian languages. Lexical deviations in Indian English as classified by Rubdy are :

1. Those, which spring from inadequate exposure to the language. These comprise :

   (a) The use of unidiomatic expressions.
   (b) The use of the wrong word owing to ignorance of the right one or uncertain recall.
   (c) The use of the wrong word out of a pair of synonyms or quasi-synonyms.
   (d) The use of high-sounding, bookish words in an attempt to sound stylistically impressive.
   (e) Malaproprisms.
   (f) Violation of selectional restrictions.
   (g) Extension of derivational processes.
   (h) Coinages.

2. Those, which are the result of a modification of the semantic range of words. These include :

   (a) Semantic extension.
   (b) Semantic restriction.
   (c) Semantic transfer.
   (d) Typical Indian English usage — uncommon in native varieties of English.

3. Those, which are a result of L2 interference:

   (a) Literal translation from L2 expressions.
   (b) Borrowings from Indian regional languages.
   (c) Hybrid word-formations.

Lexical features in Indian English are viewed not only as Indianisms, but as "manifestations of limitations in the proficiency of . . . L2 speaker of English". (Rubdy, "A Study" 273). As a sociolinguistic fact, semantic changes are caused by cultural modifications. In Indian English new meanings have been added to certain words and existent meanings have been reduced or narrowed down in others. Thus, for this, words in Indian English represent a different semantic range than they do in the language from which they are originally derived.

Collocation

Collocation is a combination of words in a language. Writers define it as the likelihood that any particular lexical item will occur in the immediate environment of another. Collocation does not involve itself to rule making or generalisation. It is learnt on an item-by-item basis. Collocation involves lexical choice between more probable and less probable lexical items. The deviant usage of collocation can be stated in terms of that which is 'more usual' and that which is 'less usual' among speakers of native English. Deviant collocations in Indian

English can be those, which are formally deviant, and those, which are contextually deviant. Members of similar objects have a similar range of collocations. Sometimes very much like objects have different range of collocations. For example, *house key, garage key, car key* are common in native English and *cycle key*, *cupboard key*, etc., in Indian English as well. The factors for deviations in collocations are :

1. Analogy and extension : (e.g., *to sport new shoes* from to sport a new bag).
2. Interchange of notionally similar words : (e.g., *put a brake to* for put an end to).
3. Pompous and high sounding words in place of simpler and more common place ones: (e.g., *consume* instead of *use/eat/drink*).
4. Fusion of two different phrases (e.g., *importance has been laid*; 'give importance to something' and 'lay emphasis/ stress on something').
5. Violation of selectional restriction : (e.g., decipher the atmosphere).
6. Interference of L1 (e.g., 'take out a procession; instead of lead a procession, give stress' instead of lay stress).
7. Indian socio-cultural context (e.g., *country wine, circle a camphor, dry day*, *sandal paste*, etc.).
8. Borrowing words from Indian languages : (e.g., *tanga driver, satyagraha movement,* etc.).

Style/Register in Indian English

Style is determined by situation and its social norms. There are mixing levels where formal and informal expressions combine to form stylistically incongruous sentences. Indian English is characterised by the following tendencies :

1. Use of slang words.
2. Combination of colloquial words with formal

expressions (e.g., *dishing out fabricated reports, exorbitant and fancy prices*).

3. Use of colloquial words and expressions (e.g., *how come*; *has given the go by*).
4. Occurrence of dated or archaic words.
5. The use of register bound (official, legal, etc.) expressions in non-registral (common) contexts.
6. Verbosity or extravagant use of words (i.e., two or more near synonym words are favouritism and nepotism, better and adequate).

10. Larry E. Smith

Larry E. Smith, discussing the use of world varieties of English, in his article on "Spread of English and Issues of Intelligibility" mentions that there is a possibility that the speakers of different varieties of English may become unintelligible to one another. English is intelligible to only those with whom we communicate in English. Larry cites an example: there may be English-speaking people in India who communicate with other Indians in English and who are not intelligible to English-speaking Filipinos who also use English to communicate with each other. The Indians and the Filipinos use English with fellow countrymen and have little or no difficulty in English communication. Then there is the question of international situations, where people wish to communicate in English. In such situations of international intelligibility, Larry poses the question as to how intelligible are speakers of different nations. He makes a pilot study on three types of subject groups : non-native, native and mixed English speakers of nine different nations. His study is based on the elements of intelligibility, comprehensibility and interpretability. He concludes intelligibility (or word/utterance recognition) is easier than comprehensibility (or word/utterance meaning) and interpretability (or meaning behind word/utterance). Language proficiency, according to the author, does not influence intelligibility, comprehensibility and interpretability but it is most important for comprehensibility. If the speakers of different varieties of English were familiar with each other's linguistic codes (particularly English), then varieties of English across cultures would be intelligible.

11. Kamal K. Sridhar and S. N. Sridhar

Kamal K. Sridhar and S. N. Sridhar in their study on Second Language Acquisition theory and 'Indigenized' varieties of English discuss differences relating to the following :

(a) *The target of acquisition:* The second-language learner in target language environments is expected to be able to use the language effectively with native speakers.
(b) *The input to the acquisition process:* The variety of English available to the learner's as primary input is the indigenous variety of English.
(c) *The role of the acquired language in relation to the other languages in the learner's repertoire:* Learners of Indigenized variety of English use English along with other languages in their repertoire. Extensive bilingualism is of importance in their acquisition and use.
(d) *Motivation of the learners*: The motivation and attitude of Indigenized variety of English learners have shown according to Willard D. Shaw that "the reasons for studying English and the skills desired are overwhelmingly the ones normally labelled instrumental."
(e) *Lexical and pragmatic aspects of Indigenized varieties of English acquisition:* Involves innovations in the lexicon, collocational possibilities, etc. ("Bridging the Paradigm Gap" 94).

As second language acquisition theory, Kamal K. Sridhar

and S. N. Sridhar point out inter-language, pidginisation, creolisation, and transfer. "Interlanguage" refers to a variety of intermediate systems between the native language and the "target" language. These are the intermediate stages in the second language learners' language; immigrant varieties, institutionalised (indigenised) non-native varieties and different types of pidgins. Inter-language is the product of a number of processes, such as, language transfer, second language learning and communication strategy, overgeneralisation of target language structures, etc. According to L. Selinker the problem in Second Language Acquisition theory is the phenomenon of *fossilization* as fossilizable phenomena are "linguistic items, rules and subsystems which speakers of a particular (native language) will tend to keep in their [interlanguage] relative to a particular (target language)" (Sridhar, "Bridging the Paradigm Gap" 98). As an example, he opines, "Indian English as an IL [interlanguage] with respect to English seems to fossilize the *that* complement or . . . *that* construction for all verbs that take sentential complements" (98).

S. N. Sridhar in his study on second language acquisition, analyses a number of non-native syntactic patterns in a specific variety (English influenced by Kannada) of Indian English. He makes interesting observations on the syntax of South Asian English. His study is based on a group of students who were in their final year of formal training in English. According to him, from the study, the lexical and syntactic patterns of non-native varieties of English show similar structures corresponding to the structures of the native language, L1 (Kannada).

Kamal K. Sridhar investigating the Pragmatics of South Asian English records how the speech acts such as informing, permitting and directing are performed in the non-native varieties of English (Indian English) and their differences from the native varieties of English. He made a pilot study on one hundred and sixty four students from three different colleges (Mount Carmel College, NMKRV College and Vijaya College) in the Bangalore city and concluded the following :

1. The majority of respondents indicated that they would not use English with (a) friend's mother in his house; (b) the waiter in a local Koshy's restaurant; and (c) a younger school boy on the street.
2. The respondents were unsure about terms of address and attention getters in different situations.
3. Respondents from all backgrounds gave long explanations justifying their request in a particular situation (Sridhar, "Pragmatics of South Asian English" 156).

Characterising the acquisitional environments of the Indianised Varieties of English, Kamal. K. Sridhar focuses on the theorising of second language acquisition. The few major differences he discusses are: (a) the target of acquisition, (b) the input to the acquisitional process, (c) the role of the acquired language in relation to other languages in the learner's repertoire, (d) motivations of the learners, and (e) lexical and pragmatic aspects of the Indian variety of English.

The second language learner in target language environments is assumed to be able to use the language effectively with native speakers. The Indianised variety of English is acquired in contexts of relatively restricted input. The learner is not exposed to the full range of styles, structures and speech acts that is normally associated with the use of language as a vehicle of communication. The model of bilingualism appropriate in the Indian variety of English is, therefore, a complementary one and not a 'replacive' or 'duplicative' model (Sridhar, *English in Indian Bilingualism* 57).

12. S. K. Verma

S. K. Verma in "Syntactic Irregularities" notes Indian English as a dialectal variety of English, which is different from American English, Australian English, British English and other mother tongue varieties of English. Describing Indianness of Indian

English, he remarks 'deviations' as 'creations,' created to find translation equivalents of concepts and ideas in Indian culture, faiths and beliefs. He examines syntactic irregularities in Indian English and notes the following features of Indian English :

1. **Inter-Clause Sequence of Tense**
   When I met him yesterday he said he is coming. [English: *When I met him yesterday he said he was coming*.]
2. **Conditional Sentences**
   If he would have worked hard, he would have passed the test. [English: *If he had worked hard, he would have passed the test*.]
3. **Indirect Questions**
   Tell me what are your jobs. [English: *Tell me what your jobs are*?]
   Do you know where does he live. [English: *Do you know where he lives*?]
   I do not know how far will it help me. [English: *I do not know how far it will help me*.]
4. **Tag Questions**
   Your friend went home yesterday, isn't it?
   [English: *Your friend went home yesterday, didn't he*?]
   You can do this work, isn't it? [English: *You can do this work, can't you*?]
   You are coming, no? [English: *You are coming, aren't you*?]
5. **Tense and Aspects**
   I have visited that place only last year. [English: *I visited that place only last year*.]
   My brother has taught at this college two years ago.
   [English: *My brother taught at this college two years ago*.]
   I am here since this morning. [English: *I have been here since this morning*.]
   He is working here since three days. [English: *He has been working here for three days*.]
   She is working as a teacher since two years. [English: *She has been working as a teacher for two years*.]

6. **Wh-Questions**
   Where you are working now? [English: *Where are you working now*?]
   What you say, Mr Singh? [English: *What do you say, Mr Singh*?]
   Why your friend has not come today? [English: *Why has your friend not come today*?]
   Wh + aux + Subject NP + MV + . . . in Indian English is rewritten as Wh + Subject NP + aux + MV +. . . .
7. **Response Type Sentences**
   Question: *Aren't you coming this evening*?
   Response: *Yes, I am not* (coming) or *No, I am* (coming) [English: Yes, I am or No, I am not.]
   Verma mentions ("Syntactic Irregularities" 214) that in English, selection of 'yes' or 'no' in a response to a question depends on the polarity of the situation. If the situation is positive, the answer is 'yes + an affirmative statement'; if the situation is negative, the answer is 'no + a negative statement.' In Indian English, as in other Indian languages, selection of 'yes' or 'no' depends on the polarity relationship between the question and the situation. If the question and the situational fact are positive, the answer is: Yes + an affirmative statement. If they are both negative, the answers are: Yes + a negative statement *or* No + a negative statement. If the form of the question is 'negative' but the situational fact is 'positive', the answers are: No + an affirmative statement *or* Yes + an affirmative statement. If the form is 'positive' and the situational fact 'negative', the answers are: Yes + a negative statement *or* No + a negative statement.
8. **Word Order**
   Your both hands are dirty. [English: *Both your hands are dirty*.]
   My all friends are here. [English: *All my friends are here*.]

In English, predeterminers (all, both, some of) occur before the possessives/articles/demonstratives. In Indian English, as in other Indian languages, they occur before and after the possessives.

The other categories discussed are 'know'-type verb in the progressive aspect, relative clauses followed by correlative pronouns and collocation.

13. Findings

A review of the earlier works on Indian English that could be consulted at the Central Institute of English and Foreign Languages, Hyderabad, and at the Indian Institute of Advanced Studies, Shimla, in addition to those available at the Indian Institute of Technology, Kanpur, and some of those on the internet shows that scholars here and abroad have been engaged in the last five decades in analysing the features of Indian English, in disambiguating, isolating, identifying elements in the phonology, lexicology and syntax of the new emerging Indian English. They had in the past, studied, Indian English from the print media and amongst students of second language learners. Scholars such as Rani Rubdy, S. V. Parasher and S. K. Verma had made a detailed study of Indian English in the areas of syntax, lexico-semantics, cohesion, grammatical and stylistic features. Studies on the stress patterns and intonation had also been made. However, so far no attempts have been made to analyse the linguistic features of Indian English from Indian English fiction since 1980 to date—a period during which a number of authors writing in Indian English have copiously contributed. Hence, this book attempts an analysis of such representative writers of the last two and a half decades.

Notes

1. Parasher (*Indian English—Functions and Form* 9) mentions that since English in India has co-existed along with other Indian languages, it in course of time has been X-ized or Indianized and as a result a non-native variety of English has come into existence.
2. 'ø' is used to indicate dropped definite/indefinite article.

Chapter - 3

Phonological Features

This chapter makes a brief review of the previous works on the phonology of Indian English and then concentrates on the phonetic characteristics (articulatory, auditory and acoustic) of some of the sounds used in Indian English. The following topics are discussed under "Phonological Features":

1. Phonetics and Phonology of Indian English
2. Variations in Vowel Utterances in Orthographic Representations
3. Indian English Pronunciation
4. Intonation and Indian English
5. Meaning in Intonation
6. Functions of Intonation
7. Findings

Kachru, Spencer, Taylor, and Gopalkrishnan on the pedagogical studies of Indian English Phonology make the first section : Phonetics and Phonology of Indian English. The variations in vowel utterances noted in some characters from Rohinton Mistry's novel *Such a Long Journey* are discussed in the subsequent section. Other Indian English pronunciation features stated by Bansal are noted in the following section. In section four, the intonation patterns of a selected list of sentences from the novel are mapped against stressed and unstressed syllables. Six factors expressing different emotional meanings from intonation are discussed in "Meaning in Intonation", and the following section identifies three functions of intonation found from the novel. The final section discusses the overall findings from the chapter.

1. Phonetics and Phonology of Indian English

Pedagogical studies on phonetics and phonology of South Asian English reveal the regional varieties of the area in which the L1 of the speaker is the demarcation point. The phonetic and phonological deviation in Indian English is generally determined by the phonetic and phonological structures of L1. According to Kachru (*Indianization* 27), these deviations are of two types, namely, (a) the segmental phonemes, and (b) the non-segmental phonemes.

The segmental phonemes : Segmental phonemes are the fundamental blocks of sound structure. In most Indian languages the CCC morpheme structure (as in English) is modified by VCC(C) morpheme structure. e.g., [*isku:l*] for *school,* [*isteiʃn*] for *station*. In Indian languages the fricatives /f, θ, ð/ do not occur as members of the phonetic system. Thus, the L2 elements are substituted by L1 elements. The fricatives are transferred by stops and the alveolar series by retroflex series in Indian English.

The non-segmental phonemes : Supra-segmental phonemes involve structure of syllables, stress and tone. The phonological features of Indian English, which demarcate the L1 varieties of English, are deviations in stress, rhythm and intonation. In this context, the observation of Spencer about the stress pattern of the Anglo-Indian speakers of English in India is relevant. Spencer remarks :

> It is . . . in certain prosodic features that the most distinctive deviation from R.P. [Received Pronunciation] is to be observed; in particular the relationship between stress, pitch and syllable length. The tendency . . . for stressed syllables . . . [is] accompanied by a fall in pitch . . . [which is] followed by a rise in the succeeding syllable, even on final unstressed syllables in statements. The tonic "accent" is accompanied by a lengthening of the syllable . . . but this lengthening usually takes the form of a doubling of the final consonant(s) before the transition to the

> following "unstressed" syllable. ("Notes on the Pronunciation" 66-67)

The L1 influence on the stress patterns of Indian English, deviations according to the study of Gopalkrishnan (L1 taken as a Dravidian language) can be summarised as the following :

1. Unawareness of the patterns of primary and secondary stress,
2. Ignorance of the stress patterns of nouns and adjectives and those of the verbs, and
3. Unawareness of the shift in stress in different parts of speech ("Some Observation" 62-67).

The non-native speakers of English tend to give stronger and equal stress to the unstressed and weak syllables of English. Their stress patterns and points of juncture tend to be unpredictable. Deviations in the stress patterns when L1 is an Indo-Aryan language, identified from the study of Taylor, are :

1. A tendency to place stress on suffix and in other instances randomly rather than where predictable on the penultimate syllable.
2. A tendency to accord weak-strong stress to nouns as well as verbs in the group of two-syllable words showing grammatical contrast through stress.
3. A general lack of recognition of the primary/tertiary pattern of stress for compound nouns as opposed to the secondary/primary pattern used with free noun/noun combination; use of secondary/primary pattern for both.
4. A strong tendency to give full value to auxiliary verb forms written as contractions, and to accord them a relatively strong stress.
5. A tendency to break up grammatical units arbitrarily within sentences, violating the confines of 'sense groups' and placing a strong stress on words other than those

normally found to have 'sense stress' (qtd. in Kachru, *English in South Asia* xxvi).

2. Variations in Vowel Utterances in Orthographic Representations

The underlying reason for such deviations is that all main South Asian languages are syllable-timed as opposed to English which is stress-timed. Rhythm in South Asian English is based not on stressed and unstressed syllables but on arranging long and short syllables. In Indian English, "all syllables in an utterance receive equal prominence and a length of time relative to the numbers of segments each contains. This characteristic is . . . 'isosyllabism' " (Kachru, *Asian Englishes* 46). For vowels there is considerable regional variation. There is no distinction between the strong and weak forms of vowels.

From Rohinton Mistry's novel *Such a Long Journey*, deviations in the phonetic characteristics of the following kinds appear. These variations are due to unfamiliarity with the Received Pronunciation utterances of the English lexical items. The deviant pronunciation is often due to borrowed English words in Indian languages and incorporation of the same variation in Indian English. The use of the word 'risvard' for 'reserved' is to be noted in the following sentences:

> " *'This is not a reserved train,' said Gustad.*"
> " *'Yes, Yes, but I will find you risvard seat'. . . said the coolie.*" (258)

Thus reserved / r i'zɜ:vd/ > risvard / r is'vɒd/ or /ɜ:/ >/ɒ/. In RP /ɒ/ is realised in *pot*, *what*, *cost* as a short back almost open vowel. RP /ɜ/ is articulated with the centre of the tongue raised between half-close and half-open, no firm contact being made between the tongue and the upper molars. The lips are neutrally spread. And the quality is, therefore, remote from all peripheral cardinal vowel values. This is shown in the conventional cardinal vowel diagram 3.1.

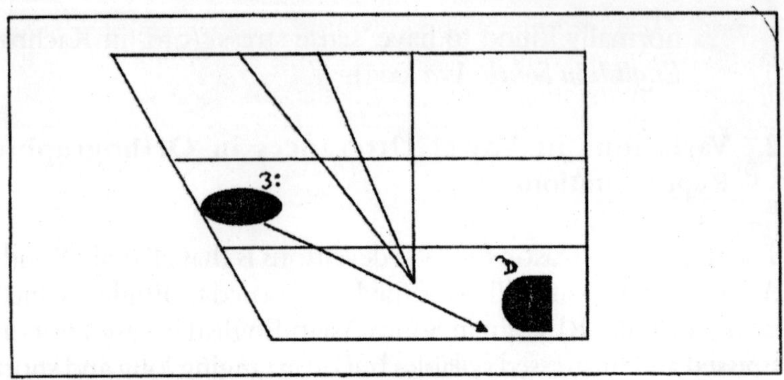

Diagram 3.1

In the following sentences 'snacks' is represented as 'snakes':

> *"The policeman said there was tea and snacks in the canteen downstairs. He pronounced it snakes."* (272)

The word snacks /snæks/ > snakes /sneiks/ or /æ/ > /ei/. /æ/, as in *pat*, *plait*, *cash*, is realised in RP as a short vowel between cardinal [ɛ] and cardinal [a]. Generally it is a monophthong but there may be diphthongal glide from that position to a more central one. In RP /ei/ the glide begins from slightly below the half-close front position and moves in the direction of RP /i/. The change is shown in the following diagram 3.2.

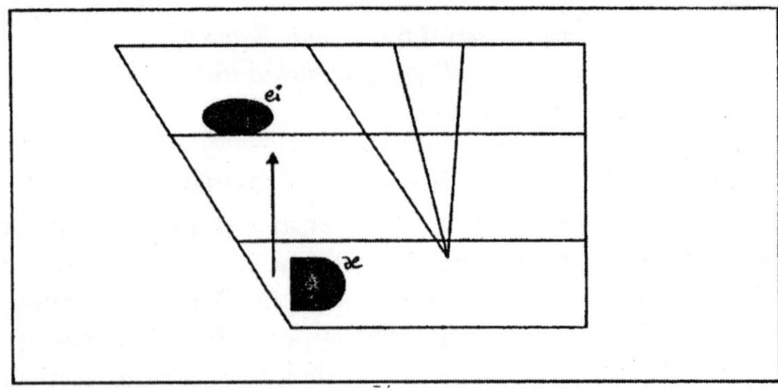

Diagram 3.2

From the phonetic changes mentioned above it can be said that the front low-mid vowel /æ/ changes into the diphthong /ei/ in the environment before the unaspirated voiceless velar consonant. For the native speaker, the new word due to a shift in pronunciation unfolds into a different word with a new meaning associated with 'the reptile'.

In the novel, there are significant phonetic divergences in the words *pop music* and *pop corn*, as they become 'pope music' and 'pope corn.' Thus /pъp'kɔ:n/ > /pəup:kɔn/, and /pъp mju:zik/ > /pəup'mju:zik/ or /ъ/ > /əu/. The glide RP /əu/ begins at a central position, between half-close and half-open and moves in the direction of RP /u/. There is a slight closing movement of the lower jaw, the lips are neutral for the first element but have a tendency to round on the second element. The change in vowel quality is shown in the following diagram 3.3.

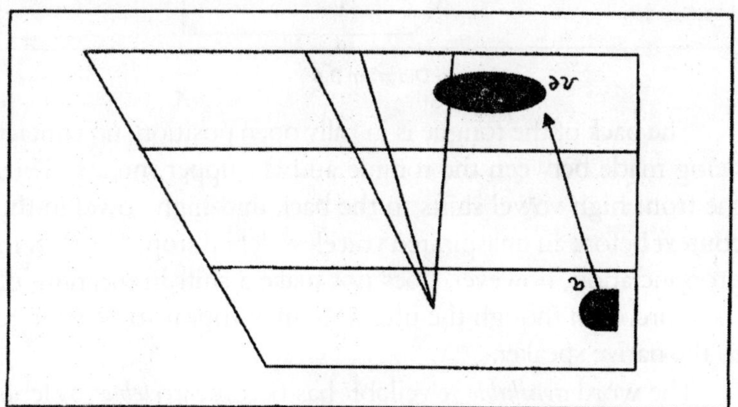

Diagram 3.3

In the above phonetic change, the back low vowel /ɒ/ changes into the diphthongal vowel glide /əu/ in the context in between unaspirated voiceless bilabial plosives. The shift in phonetic pronunciation also results in a shift of meaning to the word that is the head of the Roman Catholic Church.

Further deviations in vowel is found in the word *biscuit* /bis'kit/ which is shown as *biskoat* /bis'kot/ in the novel, that is' /i/ > /o/. RP realisation of /i/, as in *wit, mystic, village* is short and monophthongal. RP /o/ as realised in *go, both, folk, know*, is a short vowel, articulated with open lip-rounding and wide open jaws. The change is shown as in the following cardinal vowel diagram 3.4.

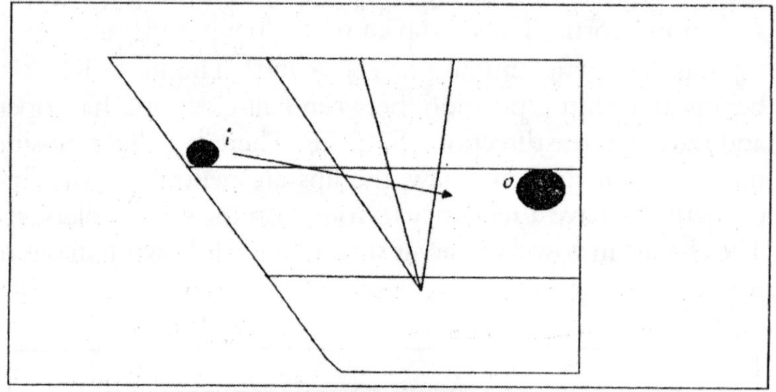

Diagram 3.4

The back of the tongue is in fully open position, no contact being made between the tongue and the upper molars. Thus the front high vowel shifts to the back mid-high vowel in the context before an unaspirated voiceless dental stop. The shift in pronunciation, however, does not make a shift in meaning of the word even though the utterance may appear to be strange to the native speaker.

The word *available* /e'veiləbl/ has become *aveleble* /əv'lebl/ or /eɪ/ > /i/. In RP, /ei/ is generally realised in, e.g., *day, late, vein* as a diphthong moving from a position between cardinals [e] and [ɛ] to a typical RP [ɪ] position. The change is shown in diagram 3.5. The change of quality is not very great but usually perceptible. In the above accent, the sound is a monophthong. The phoneme /i:/ found in *see, unique, receive*, has a monophthongal realisation.

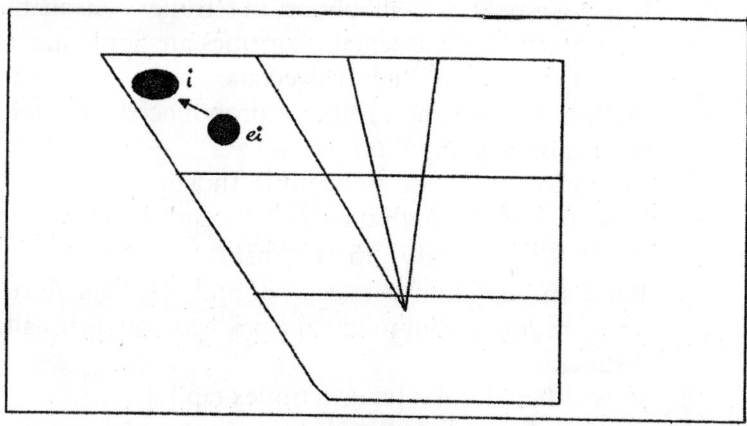

Diagram 3.5

In India there are many languages with their own inflection and intonation, which do not approximate the language spoken by the British. A number of educated Indians often confuse 'pronunciation' with 'accent'. It is assumed that anyone who speaks good, idiomatic and flawless English speaks with an accent. But in the English speaking world anyone who is said to be speaking with an 'accent' would be considered half-educated, if not illiterate (Pandit, "Thick Indian Accent" 2006). Deviant pronunciation of words termed as standard Indian English remains comparatively unknown and unacceptable to the rest of the world. In multi-syllable words attention is not paid to placing stress on the right syllable.

3. Indian English Pronunciation

English is the third most widely spoken language in the world today. There are variations in pronunciations affected by native language, educational background and contact with English. Fast speech-tempo with choppy syllables, rhythmic variation in pitch and stress on the verb in questions are Indian English features. The following are Indian English phonetic features :

1. English alveolars are perceived by Indic and Dravidian

language speakers as allophones of retroflex consonants whereas the Indian dental phonemes are approximate equivalents to the English alveolars.

2. Diphthongs /eɪ / and /ou/ are pronounced monophthongally as /e:/ and /o:/.
3. Confusion of /p/ and /f/ by north Indians.
4. Low back vowel /ɒ/ fronted to /a/ except when followed by /θ/ ('bath' /baθ/, 'mark' /mak/).
5. Random alteration between /æ/ and /e/; 'bat' /bæt/, 'mess' as /mæs/. But minimal pairs 'bed-bad' is usually distinct.
6. /r/ is either alveolar [r] or retroflex tap [r].
7. In north India, epenthetic vowels /i, ə/ tend to precede the clusters /sp, st, sk/; 'speak' /ispi:k/, etc.

According to the previous studies by R. K. Bansal on Indian English pronunciation and studies from Indian English contemporary fiction it can be mentioned that many Indian speakers do not know that their pronunciation scheme deviates from RP. In general, the following are the deviant phonological features between Indian English and Received Pronunciation :

1. All native languages of India lack the voiced palatal or post alveolar sibilant /dǯ/, as in 'treasure'.
2. Indian English lacks the difference between /v/, voiced labio-dental fricative and /w/, velar semi-vowel. Most Indians use a frictionless labio-dental approximant close to /v/ for both /v/ and /w/ graphemes. So *wine* is pronounced as *vine*.
3. Generally Indian English lacks the phonemes /θ/ voiceless dental fricative and /ð/ voiced dental fricative. Hence, the aspirated voiceless dental plosive /th/ is substituted as /θ/ and the unaspirated voiced dental plosive /d/ is substituted for /ð/. On being heard by native speakers, this can create confusion.

4. In RP word initial and syllable initial /p/, /t/, /k/ is slightly aspirated. In most Indian languages unlike English, the distinction between aspirated and unaspirated plosives is phonemic. So Indian English in such contexts, uses the corresponding unaspirated voiceless plosives /p/, /t/, /k/ instead of /ph/, /th/ and /kh/.
5. A deviant feature of Indian English is the use of retroflex plosives /T/, /D/ in place of the corresponding alveolar plosives of English /t/ and /d/.
6. English is a stress-timed language and word stress is an important feature of English pronunciation. Indian English speakers either put the stress accent on the wrong syllable or accentuate all the syllables of a long English word. The English spoken by Indian English speakers has a peculiar pitch accent which makes it to the native speaker's ear in a sing-song tone.
7. In most native Indian languages, there are no affricates. So Indian pronunciation of RP affricates /tʃ/ and /dʒ̆/ are as corresponding palatal plosives without the following friction.
8. Syllabic /l/ /m/ /n/ are usually replaced by voiced consonant clusters.
9. Many Indian speakers fail to make a clear distinction between /e/ and /ɛ/ and /ъ/ and /ɔ/ (*cot-caught*).
10. As against RP /ʌ/, /ə/ and /ɜ/, the areas for /ə/ and /ɜ/ overlap (Bansal, *The Intelligibility* 121), and /ɜ/ does not exist in the speech of many Indians. In Indian English, only /ə/ occurs.
11. /r/ in RP occurs only before a vowel but Indian English uses a sharp alveolar trill /r/ in all word positions. Indian speakers do not use the retroflex approximant for /r/.

4. Intonation and Indian English

Intonation is related to the perception of pitch, that is, the frequency of the vibration of air molecules set in motion during speech. Intonation is also a type of melodic approach to the accented syllable, for example, steep versus gradual pitch movement. The basic unit of intonation is the tone-unit, a stretch of utterance with major pitch movements and at least one prominent syllable. The constituents of the tone-unit are the nucleus, the head, the pre-head and the tail. The nucleus is a prominent syllable in a tone-unit. Its prominence is due to "the presence of noticeable pitch movement, either in the form of a glide on the nuclear syllable or in the form of a jump from the nuclear syllable to the following syllables" (Couper-Kuhlen, *An Introduction to English Prosody* 79). The head, sometimes called 'body' extends from the first stressed syllable to the nucleus. The first rhythmically stressed syllable of the head is the onset. The pre-head consists of all the unstressed syllables which precede the head. These are few in number, the maximum being five. The tail is defined as any stressed or unstressed syllable following the nucleus.

According to Elizabeth Couper-Kuhlen, *An Introduction to English Prosody* 78, the terms of component structure of a tone-unit are:

		nucleus	
	head	nucleus	
	head	nucleus	tail
pre-head	head	nucleus	
pre-head		nucleus	
pre-head		nucleus	tail
		nucleus	tail
pre-head	head	nucleus	tail

From the novel *Such a Long Journey* the intonation patterns of the sentences were analysed intuitively as follows. The dots stand for separate syllables. Larger ones represent nuclei and the smaller ones are heads, pre-heads and tails. The intonation patterns of the sentences and phrases in italics, taken up for analysis from the novel were made purely intuitively with the help of a Gujarati-Sindhi speaking U.G. science student.[1]

A. "*Come on, get up ! He got admission !*" (7)

B. "Gustad wanted to wake Sohrab. Dilnavaz stopped him. 'Let him sleep. *His admission result is not going to change if he knows one hour later*'." (8)

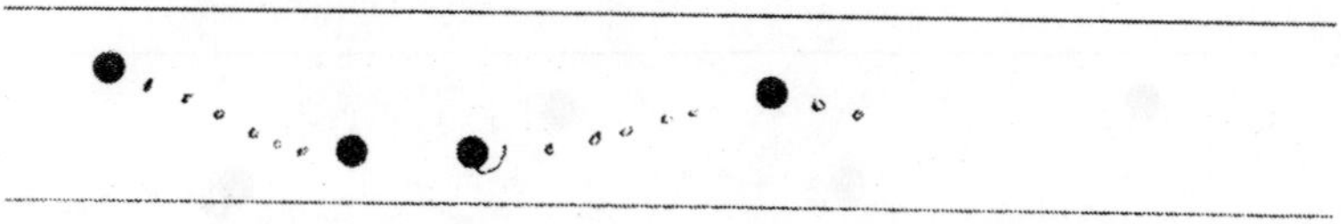

C. " '*Wait, I am filling the maltoo*,' she said, unable to hear over the gush of running water." (12)

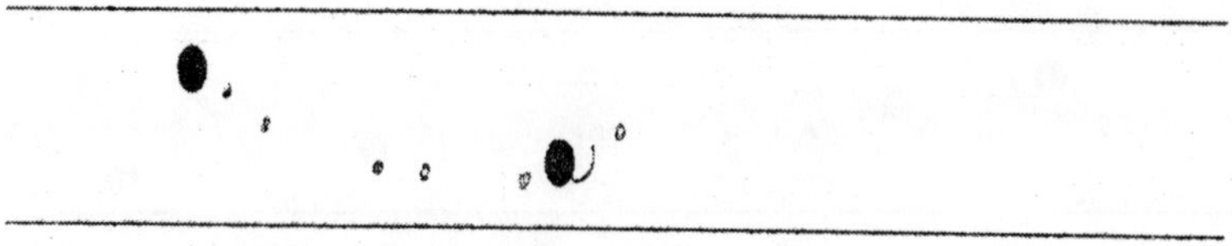

D. " '*Where did we get this basket from anyway*?' asked Gustad, covering the chicken with the wide wicker basket that had hung for ages on a nail near the kitchen ceiling."(18)

E. " '*I'm not going to touch the chicken*,' snapped Dilnavaz. If he thought she could be tricked into looking after the creature, he was sadly mistaken." (20)

F. "*Sohrab and I will make that bookcase one of these days,* then all the books and papers will fit in nicely. OK, Sohrab?" (27)

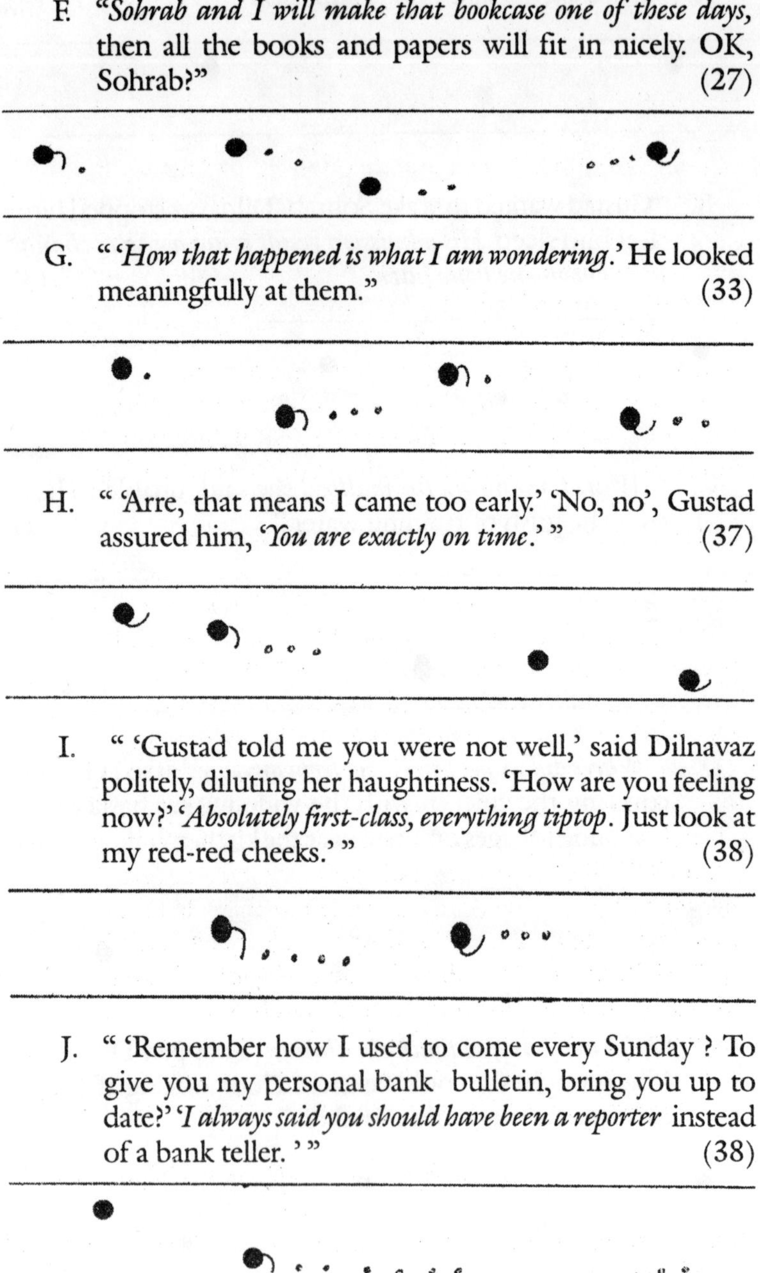

G. " '*How that happened is what I am wondering*.' He looked meaningfully at them." (33)

H. " 'Arre, that means I came too early.' 'No, no', Gustad assured him, '*You are exactly on time*.' " (37)

I. " 'Gustad told me you were not well,' said Dilnavaz politely, diluting her haughtiness. 'How are you feeling now?' '*Absolutely first-class, everything tiptop*. Just look at my red-red cheeks.' " (38)

J. " 'Remember how I used to come every Sunday ? To give you my personal bank bulletin, bring you up to date?' '*I always said you should have been a reporter* instead of a bank teller.' " (38)

K. "Before either Sohrab or Dilnavaz could respond, a shrill cry rang out. '. . . This is sleeping-time, not fighting-time. *Save the rest for the morning!*' " (51)

L. " 'Gustad said no with his hand, 'Going for a walk.' '*I'll also come. I can eat walking-walking*. Good for stomach and digestion.' " (72)

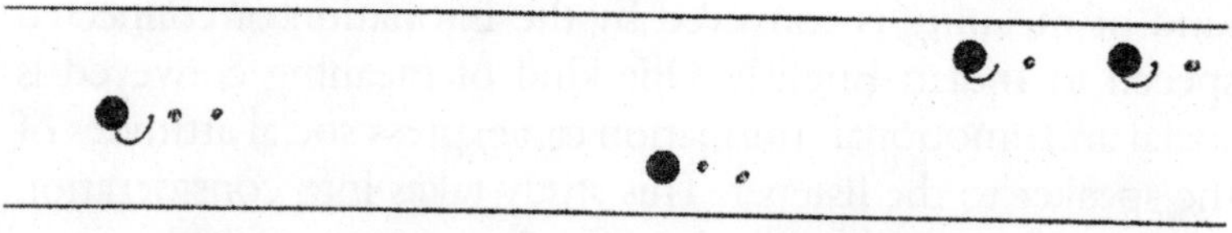

M. "Fair or not fair, I don't care. *I don't want the dogwalla idiot complaining again*. Discussion over. Let's have dinner." (79)

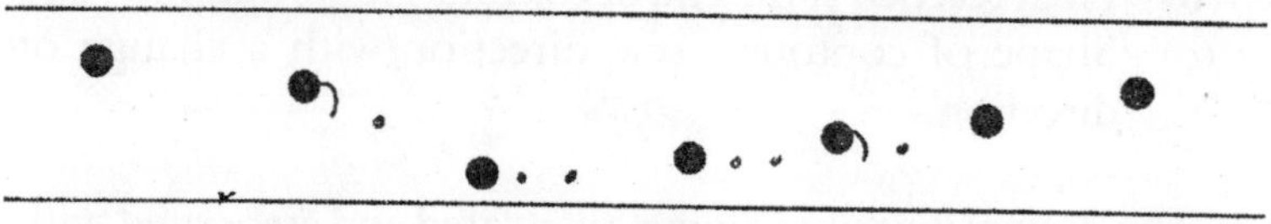

N. " 'Come in,' she said, 'if he is still at the bus stop I'll call him back.' 'No, no, no. How can I give so much trouble?' '*It's OK, bus stop is just outside the compound.*' " (188)

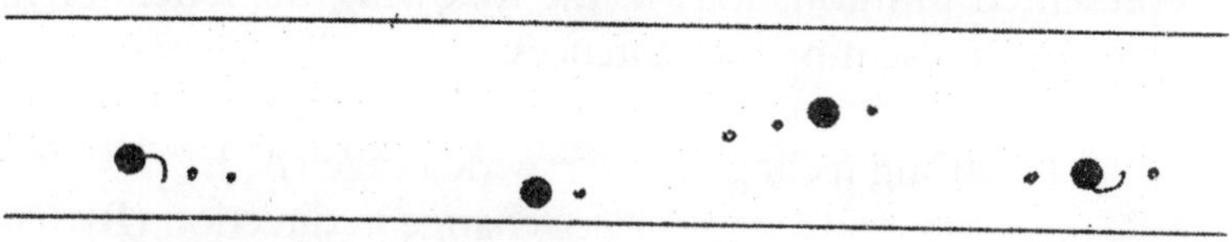

O. " '*Whatever you wish. You know best,* . . . ' She thanked her humbly and left." (207)

P. " '. . . Now leave it till sunrise under the bed where Sohrab used to sleep. Below the head. And bring it back tomorrow.' '*Then what happens* ?' 'One step at a time. Do this much first.' " (276)

---

5. Meaning in Intonation

Generalising over the sixteen extracts, it is obvious that some kind of meaning is conveyed by the intonation of connected speech in Indian English. One kind of meaning conveyed is social and emotional. Intonation can express social attitudes of the speaker to the listener. This study takes into consideration the following variables for the different contours of intonation :

(a) Range : wide/narrow;
(b) Pitch reached at the end of contour : high/mid/low; and
(c) Shape of contour : one direction/with a change of direction.

The dimensions of meaning postulated and associated with contour variation in the study are mapped (Uldall, "Dimensions of Meaning in Intonation," 258) against six factors (expressing dimensions of emotional meaning which are strongly represented in intonation) in the following the letters of the alphabet representing the sentences.

1. 'strong feeling'	wide range (A, E)
	change in direction (B)
2. 'authoritative'	raised weak syllable (J)
	raised ending in the mid (H)
	raised ending at the end (C)
	change of direction (D)
3. 'unpleasant'	raised ending high (F)

4. 'pleasant'	lowered weak syllable (G)
	raised ending high (M)
	raised weak syllable (K)
5. 'submissive'	raised ending (L, O)
	raised ending in the mid (N)
	narrow range (P)
6. 'feeble'	raised weak syllable (I)

The study shows that the contour for unpleasant factor is raised ending while those for the pleasant factor are lowered weak syllable, raised high ending and raised weak syllable. The contours for the two factors thus vary in the ratio 1:3 in the unpleasant and pleasant sector. The question-word questions (P, D) appear in the authoritative and submissive sectors only. The contours which are mostly neutral in various sentence types are: statements in final raised ending in mid-pitch, command in high ending and question-word question in high ending or mid-syllabic contour.

6. Functions of Intonation

(i) Attitudinal Function

In attitudinal functions of intonation the surprised question '*Where did we get this basket from*?' has wide pitch range and steep rising and falling in the utterance. However in Indian languages there are similar means for expressing such nuances of meaning. In the above example, the question-word question has a higher pitch on *where* and a steeper falling pitch curve. 'Surprise,' 'exasperation,' and 'impatience' can be thought of as attitudes. Speakers make real-time assessment of what words need to be stressed, or what attitude or intention they wish to convey by means of intonation.

(ii) Discourse Function

The answer-statements '*It's OK, bus stop is just outside the compound. Just come in and sit baba*' are examples of discourse function of intonation which illustrate contrast and emphasis through intonation and the importance of the surrounding context of discourse and the expectations of the hearer and the speaker. In this case the speaker informs the hearer that she or someone else will go to the bus stop and possibly expects that the hearer will be surprised to find out that the speaker or someone else is going to the bus stop. Like Indian languages, stress on the word 'just' implies duration of a few seconds.

(iii) Grammatical Function

This is the "neutral" utterance typically used to illustrate grammatical functions of intonation; e.g., 'You are exactly on time.' It is interesting to note that all three utterances have similar intonation patterns, typical of English statements. They show pitch peaks on stressed syllables with the greatest peak on the syllable with sentence stress. At the end of the utterance, the pitch falls to its lowest level. In this case there is no one-to-one correspondence between intonation pattern and sentence type.

7. Findings

The vowel shifts of English words in Indian English can be formulated as:

(1) /з/ ——→ /ɒ/ (environment unspecifiable as there is change in vowel position, reserved / r i'z3:vd/ > risvard / r ɪs' vɒd/);
(2) /æ/——→ /ei/ / n—k / #;
(3) /ъ/——→ /əu/ / p—p / #; and
(4) /i/——→ /o/ / k—t / #.

From the study on the data from the novel, it can be said that the factors illuminating the three dimensions of meaning in intonation patterns in Indian English are: (i) strong/weak, (ii) authoritative/submissive, and (iii) pleasant/unpleasant.

In the Chapter, different patterns of sound from Indian English novels are discussed according to segmental and supra-segmental phonology. This chapter provides a general frame-work for the phonological structure of the language. The study is based on specific observations on the language dealing with the phonological patterns of declaratives, answer phrases, questions and assertives. The deviations in Indian English pronunciation discussed in section 3 exist because Indians tend to look at their own rich phonology for the nearest approximation of English phonemes and then, like most Indian native language pronunciation, follow English pronunciation as it appears through the English spelling. However, as a matter of fact, most foreigners still consider Indians to be much better speakers of good English than most other people including the Chinese, the Japanese, the Italian or the French.

Note

1. Ms. Ekta Makhija, a UG course student helped me in preparing the "Intonation and Indian English" section.

Chapter - 4

Lexical Features

There are words and expressions of Indian origin in Indian English fiction. This chapter focuses on these characteristic lexical features in the works of Indian English fiction of the nineteen eighties and nineties. This period is chosen because in these two decades many authors of Indian Writing in English (IWE) began their careers and gained recognition for their work. As early as 1886, works in the field of lexical analysis with ethnographic, socio-political, administrative and descriptive characteristics are noted in *Hobson-Jobson*, which is a glossary of colloquial Anglo-Indian words and phrases and of kindred terms, with etymological, historical, geographical and discursive details. Another register oriented study is *A Glossary of Judicial and Revenue Terms* compiled by H. H. Wilson.

The reasons for adoption of Indian words in the language are varied. G. Subba Rao notes in his *Indian Words in English* that Indian words represent objects and actions for which English names cannot easily be found. They are also chosen for their picturesqueness and for imparting local colour. In this context, the following are discussed in this chapter :

1. Kinds of Borrowing
2. Classification of Borrowed Words
3. Semantic Changes in Word Formation
4. Borrowed Words from *A Suitable Boy*
5. Words of Indian Origin from *Midnight's Children*
6. Findings

From the Indian words and expressions in English language, this chapter focuses on two novels written in the nineties and eighties, namely, Vikram Seth's *A Suitable Boy* and Salman

Rushdie's *Midnight's Children*. In these two novels, there are about three hundred and fifty Indian words, nearly half of which are from Hindi and Urdu. There is also a large scale of borrowing from other languages including Bengali, Gujarati, Marathi, Malayalam and Sanskrit in the writings of other well known Indian authors such as Arundhati Roy, Rohinton Mistry, Amitav Ghosh, Upamanyu Chatterjee, and Vikram Chandra. However, it is interesting to note that most of these borrowings from other languages occurred significantly in the last two decades.

1. Kinds of Borrowing

In the area of the lexicon, Indian English exhibits expansion. Kamal K. Sridhar notes that this expansion observed by Kachru and Bokamba "is effected through several processes including heavy borrowing from native languages, calques, hybrid words and compounds, novel collocations not attested in native varieties, and neologisms created by the application of regular word-formation rules of the reference language" (qtd. in Sridhar, "Sociolinguistic Theory" 42). From Indian English novels the following four types of borrowing are found :

(i) Loan Words

This is a common mechanism where there is straight borrowing from Indian languages. These are mostly incorporated in the language because of their wide currency, brevity and ease of pronunciation. These also function as idioms in some sense, for example, *jayamala (ASB 7), purdah (M's C 34), ekadashi (ASB 36), samdhin (ASB 177), zamindar (ASB 217), parishad (M's C 206), dharma (M's C 122)*, *burkha (ASB 89)* and *hartal (M's C 33)*.

(ii) Blending

Blending of borrowed expression, that is, a process whereby a non-English word is used along with an English word, which is nativised in course of time. Kachru observes that there is a certain structural and contextual constraint on blended items. For example, in the expression *lathi-charge* the Indian word *lathi* cannot be substituted by another expression. Other examples are *sajjo-soap (SALJ 56)* for good soap (*sajjo* is 'good' in Gujarati), *tandorosti-prayer (SALJ 56)* for deep prayer, *doctor-i-attache (M's C 19)* for doctor's bag, *chugha-coat (M's C 16)* for a coat of goat's skin, *chaprassi-hand (M's C 33)* for servant's hand, *green chutney (M's C 209)* for a food item made out of coriander leaves, *sherbet-stand (AFB 7)* for a drink stand, *minister-sahib (ASB 796)* for minister sir, *rickshaw-walla (M's C 52)* for a rickshaw puller, *vayudoot-office (TLB 3)* for electricity office, *jatava-caste (ASB 99)* for a high caste and *chokra-boy (TSL 25)* for a young boy. However, there are expressions where elements are interchangeable, for example, *police chowki* for police station, *mazdoor union* for labour union, *rice thali* for rice plate (a plate of meal where rice is the main item), and *kitab centre* for book centre.

(iii) Loan Translation

Loan translation is a language shift that is responsible for lexical innovations in the language. An analysis of the vocabulary from the Indian English novels shows that loan translation helps in coining new expressions in Indian English, for example, *daily passengeri (THT 4)*, *filmi music (THT 38)*, *day-labourers (AFB 259)*, *June rain (TGOST 10)*, *go-go bag (TGOST 4)*, *street Arabs (M's C 73)*, *tiffin carrier (M's C 202)*, *actual foreigner (DD 32)*, *very very late (LALIB 45)*, *understanding of the village (LALIB 260)*, *passing of the application (LALIB 49)*, etc.

(iv) Loan Creation

The process of loan creation has brought new expressions that are used in Indian English fiction. These expressions are created to manipulate Indian concepts. Many of them like *goonda-giri (AFB 520)*, *gunda-gardi*, *goondas (SALJ 39)*, *karma-yogi (ASB 549)*, *dharma-chakra (M's C 122)*, *ratnagharbha (TLB 194)*, *kada ar bada (THT 51)*, *haddi-phaelwan (M's C 214)*, *bukbuking (TSL 25)*, *chutneyfication (M's C 456)*, have been established in Indian English primarily through newspaper usage.

2. Classification of Borrowed Words

From the classification of borrowed words in the last two decades it is found that the number of words borrowed is larger than those in the1960s and the1970s. Also the distribution of the new words is remarkably unequal, that is, for those of the first half of the twentieth century are few while the large majority belongs to the latter half. This is for the fact that other than Mulk Raj Anand, Raja Rao and R. K. Narayan, who started their writing careers in the 1920s and the 1930s, most of the new writers started writing in the latter half of the century.

In the twentieth century, India's struggle for independence adopted uncommon words such as *Ghandhism*, *hartal*, *khaddar*, *khilafat*, *satyagraha*, *swadeshi*. Indian words adopted into English have fitted well into its grammatical system. Nouns constitute the largest class. In languages like Hindi and Urdu all nouns are either masculine or feminine. As observed by G. Subba Rao, 'roti' (a food item) is feminine and 'cha' (tea) masculine; 'chitty' (letter) feminine and 'tamasha' (joke) masculine. Thus they differ accordingly in their inflection and syntactic environment. These words when adopted in English inevitably ignore this gender distinction. Adjectives from Indian languages are also borrowed but they are small in number. For example, Bengali 'kacha' (unripe) and 'pukka' (ripe). "In Hindi, adjectives ending in *a* change *a* into *i* before all feminine nouns and into *e* before all masculine nouns in the plural and in the oblique cases. Thus *kachcha* (*cutcha*) takes the form *kachchi* before *chitti*" (*Indian Words in English* 51). These distinctions are not retained in English and the uninflected forms are taken over. Indian verbs are adopted in large numbers even though not many are found in works of fiction. It is significant that earlier Indian verbs in English were adopted in the imperative form and converted into the infinitive. H. Yule and A. C. Burnell observe that

"Hindustani verbs . . . are habitually adopted into the quasi-English by converting the imperative into an infinitive. Thus to *bunow*, to *lugow*, to *foozilow*, to *puckarow* . . . to *sumjow*, and so on almost *ad libitum*, are formed as we have indicated" and continue to say that "this doubtless exemplifies some obscure linguistic law" (*Hobson-Jobson* xx). Besides direct borrowings as noted above, new forms are created in English from the material borrowed by means of derivation. The examples here are from Indian English fiction though, some of these are recorded in the *Oxford English Dictionary*, and also some other examples are noted in G. Subba Rao's *Indian Words in English*.

(i) Derivative Nouns

(a) *Nouns formed by the addition of suffixes as:*

- *-age* : dacoitage
- *-dom* : baboodom, pariahdom, thugdom
- *-ism* : babuism, Brahminism, Budhhism, Hinduism, swadeshism, swarajism, vedantism, goondaism
- *-ship* : punditship, swarajship, rajahship, ameership
- *-jaan* : abbajaan, bhaijaan, chachajaan, nanajaan, phuphajaan
- *-walla* : basketwalla, box-wallah, cobrawalla, Congresswalla, dhotiwalla, dubbawalla, goaswalla, jaripuranawalla, madhiwalla, paanwalla, rickshaw-walla, sarangiwalla, tongawalla, box-walli, kuchrawalli
- *-sahib* : Bilgrami sahib, choteesahib, German sahib, khansahib, kapoor sahib, dagh sahib, ministersahib, Maan sahib, memsahib, Nawabsahib, burresahib, ustad sahib, vakilsahib, vilayat sahib, Bajaj saab, collectorsaab, rehman-shaheb
- *-ji* : ammaji, babaji, baoji, bhenji, bibiji, Dinshawji, guruji, jijaji, Lakshmanji, mamaji,

masterji, mataji, musaji, nanaji, pabiji, Panditji, phenji, pitaji, Ramchandraji, taiji, Tandonji, sadhuji, Sharmaji, Thomasji

-babu : Biswas babu, burra babu, kana-babu, Kanai babu, Naresh-babu, ukil-babu

(b) *Nouns formed by other suffixes:* brahmanhood, Indianist, Sanskritist, looter, swarajist, thuster, gunda-gardi, chutney-fication

(c) *Nouns formed by the plural suffix –s:* ballishtabs, barfis, bhotbhotis, chapattis, chappals, dalpuris, durwans, gazals, gharries, ikkas, kababs, kachuris, laddus, luchis, musammis, pakoras, parathas, puris, sadhikas, samosas, saris, sollishtahs, taluqdars, tongas, tindas

(d) *Verbal substantives formed from the verb by the addition of the suffix –ing:* being-being, fetching-fetching, head-cushioning, fighting-bighting, keep telling, killing-killing, looking-looking, looting, running-running, salaaming, shampooing, wetting, poking and pushing

(ii) ***Kinship Terms :*** amma, ammai, ammi, ammu, ammachi, ammaven, appoi, baba, babu, bhai, bhabhi, chachen, chachi, chetan, cheduthi, dada, jethamosai, ma, mammachi, pappachi, phupha, thakuma

(iii) ***Compound Nouns:*** asmai-kasmai, betel-chewers, bus-bhajan, chugha-pocket, dharma-chakra, dhobi-ghat, dhuti-panjabi, haddi-phaelwan, hakimi medicine, kathakali dancer, karma-yogi, kunukku earrings, kurta-pyjama, lathi-charge, nimbu-pani, Mu-i-Mubarak, sitam-zareef, sherbet-stand, street-arabs, thela-gari, tissue-patola sari

(iv) ***Derivative Adjectives:*** lootable, bungaloid, brahmanic, lusibari, bon bibi, bujuvea nationalists, Hindustanish

(v) ***Past Participle Used as Adjective:*** Aryanized, chhele-chhokra, jungled, khaki-turbaned, hennaed-hand

(vi) ***Derivative Verbs:*** aryanize, sanskritize, Hinduize

(vii) ***Attributive Use of Nouns:*** Nouns borrowed from the Indian languages are employed in an attributive sense to a remarkable extent in the second half of the twentieth century. The historical and cultural relations of two races dissimilar in their ways of life and thought have not hindered the adoption of Indian words. The attributive uses of the nouns are found in the following words: neel darvaza, peshwari chappals, chaprassi-hand, haddi-phaelwan, silver thali, betel chewers, pathan turbans.

(viii) ***Particles, Interjections:*** ar ki, array, arre, arre wah, arrey, are moshai, hoi-hoi, -re, oi-je, tai naki

(ix) ***Verbs Used as Nouns :*** shampoo, toco, dekko, panick, puja, gunda-giri

(x) ***Nouns Used as Verbs:***bahadur, baksheesh, curry, dacoit, palankeen, punkah, salaam

(xi) ***Use of Indian Phrases :*** Achha, choop kore thako, athero bhatir desh, bal to re, bulbul-e-din, du char jane utari aauu-dhakka lagaauu, jay thayu tay thayu, ki korcho tumi, peri pauna, pista-ki-lauz, punnyan kunju, sundarikutty, sub kuch tick tock hai, umcha section nai, tarbuz ka bazaar, uth jag musafir, takht-e-sulaiman

3. Semantic Changes in Word Formation

A number of Indian words in English have undergone semantic changes. The common processes in the semantic changes are generalisation, specialisation, transference and degeneration of senses. These processes from Indian English fiction are discussed below.

(i) Generalisation

The phenomenon of generalisation or expansion of meaning is found in the following Indian words from Indian English fiction. 'Koh-i-noor,' the famous Indian diamond has been put to figurative use; "She remembered that long ago she had shown Baby Kochamma a copy of her father's will in which, describing his grandchildren he had written: *I have seven jewels one of which is my koh-i-noor*" (*The God of Small Things* 25); 'Kumbhkaran,' a character of the Ramayana, who sleeps for six months, in a year and is awake for the rest six, is used as a generalisation to denote someone who is asleep for long hours at odd times; " 'Why did you miss last night?' demanded Bhaskar, who had been promoted tonight to be Angad, a monkey-prince . . . . 'I was asleep,' said Maan. 'Asleep! You are like Kumbhkaran,' said Bhaskar. 'You missed the best part of the battle' " (*A Suitable Boy* 1045). 'Jaadu-mantra,' magic spell or influence, is used to perform stage tricks. In the following extract it has been used for an explanation for someone's (Shorab's) improper behaviour: " 'You are saying that suddenly he does not want to study at this IIT place?' Miss Kutpitia narrowed her eyes as Dilnavaz nodded. 'And up to now he wanted to go, no one forced him?' . . . . In that case, only one thing is possible . . . . Definitely jaadu-mantra" (*Such a Long Journey* 63).

(ii) Specialisation

The process of specialisation is closely associated with generalisation. In this process a word moves from one set of circumstances to another, and thereby becomes more specialised in meaning. The following words illustrate specialisation of meaning. In the first case there has been a transfer from general sense to restricted sense while in the second case it is just the opposite. Here, it is from a restricted sense to a general sense. 'Nawab,' the title of certain Mohammedan officials who were appointed deputy governors of provinces or districts in the Mughal empire, has been used and restricted in transferred and general sense of a rich and pampered person. Chotee Nawab, Nawab sahib, occur several times in this restricted sense in *A Suitable Boy* (102). Similarly, 'Babu' in Anglo-Indian, used in the restricted sense, was a native clerk or official who writes

English. Later the word is used in transferred and general sense as a form of address to the first or last name of a man, especially an eastern Indian, who belongs to a social superior or elite group. This word also occurs in this generalised sense in *A Suitable Boy.* 'Pundit' originally signifying a priest who performs for the Hindu religious rituals, subsequently refers to a learned man who is an authority on a subject, and is also used as a title for a north Indian classical musician (both vocal and instrumental). The corresponding word in Urdu is 'ustad.' The word is used in all three senses in *A Suitable Boy*. For example, ". . . the time that the pandits have given is coming up, and there is no sign of either bride or groom!" (4); " 'Panditji means well,' said someone" (261) and "After a while the pandit told his younger assistant to take over" (1221).

(iii) Transference

Some Indian words have been figuratively used as objects or actions other than the usual ones due to some association or similarity between them. 'Walla' is a suffix in Hindi which along with substantives forms adjectives with the sense 'pertaining to' or 'connected with.' It is commonly comprehended as a substantive equivalent to 'man,' 'fellow,' as, 'dubbawalla' or tiffin box carrier in the sentence: "At lunch-time, Gustad did not go to the stairwell where the dubbawalla deposited the tiffin boxes" (*Such a Long Journey* 70). 'Purdah' (curtain) is figuratively applied to the system of seclusion by curtain. In the following extract from *A Suitable Boy*, the word occurs in this transferred sense 'the world of purdah.' ". . . she asked him about his eldest child, his daughter Zainab, who was a childhood friend of hers but who, after her marriage, had disappeared into the world of purdah" (20). Similar interpretation for the word is found in the following extract from *Midnight's Children*:

> Major Latif . . . devised her famous, all-concealing, white silk chadar, the curtain or veil . . . behind which she sat . . . . The chadar of Jamila Singer was held up

> by two tireless, muscular figures, also veiled from head to foot . . . at its very centre, the Major had cut a hole. Diameter: three inches. Circumference: embroidered in finest gold thread . . . . Jamila sang with her lips pressed against the brocaded aperture (313).

In *Midnight's Children* Rushdie has also mentioned the word "purdah" as in "He has told her to come out of purdah" (34).

(iv) Degeneration

Some Indian words have undergone degeneration of meaning in English which were first used in a debased sense. 'Pariahs,' for instance, are the largest of the lower castes in southern India. In English the word 'pariah' is applied to one who is a social outcaste. In this sense, the word is found in the following extract :

> "When the British came to Malabar, a number of Paravans, Pelayas and Pulayas converted to Christianity. . . . As a special favour they were given their own separate Pariah Bishop" (*The God of Small Things* 74).

In Anglo-Indian colloquial use 'bahaudur' denoted 'a haughty or pompous person, who exercised his authority with a strong sense of his own importance' (from the entry 'Bahaudur' in 'Hobson-Jobson,' p.48 of the Wordsworth Classics edition). Rai Bahadur is an honorary title given to the officers for their support to the British Raj. With the departure of the Britishers from India, the word today has lost its original meaning. It is no more used for a person who supported the British Raj. As in the following example 'Rai Bahadur' is used just as the title of a person: "Veena . . . was free to do as she pleased: to go to the market, to walk around by herself, to go for music lessons. For a daughter-in-law from the house of the Rai Bahadur to be seen in the market would have been disgraceful. . . . Also she (Priya) liked the ancient Rai Bahadur, her grandfather-in-law" (*ASB* 239).

(v) The Interjection 'Arrey'

One of the most common linguistic expressions of emotion in most of the languages which are descendants of Sanskrit is the conventional word 'Arrey' spelled variously by different Indian authors (with a Sanskrit offshoot as L1) writing in English. It is pronounced differently depending on the emotion expressed by the phrase following it, from a short outburst for anger or frustration to a lengthy long-drawn tapering sound indicating intimacy or affection. The following are some of the expressions of emotion it can accompany :

(a) *intimacy/affection—*
"Arrey, I shall be honoured bhai, honoured" (*English, August* 41).
"It was April, so the river was low and the current sluggish. Kabir cupped his hands and shouted: 'Are, mallah!' " (*A Suitable Boy* 163)
Here the interjection is used in the context of a friendly and familiar situation.

(b) *non-agreement/anger, frustration—*
"Aray go! Who are you to tell me?" (*A Fine Balance* 424)
"Arrey, but which Principal would'nt listen to Bajaj saab?" (*English, August* 87)
"Arrey, where to go? . . . there is so much to do in the house" (*Difficult Daughters* 36).
The context here is one of confrontation, discord.

(c) *discovery/surprise—*
"Arrey, August, you eat fish like a Bengali" (*English, August* 107).
" 'Arre wah!' exclaimed Lajwanti, clearing her throat ..." (*Difficult Daughters* 146).
"Arre, that means I came too early" (*Such a Long Journey* 37).
" 'Kanai? Is that you?' 'Are tumi!' " (*The Hungry Tide* 17)

The situation is one of bewilderment, that is, the speaker learns something previously unknown to him.

(d) *declaration/assertion*—
"Arrey, Sen, there is no pleasure like going home" (*English, August* 143).
" 'Arre', exclaimed her cousin patting her on the back, 'times are changing, and women are moving out of the house, . . . ' " (*Difficult Daughters* 16)
The context goads the speaker to say something solemnly.

(e) *expostulation*—
"Arre, where is the harm in these decorative things? Just think how it will soothe to look at a fountain splashing in the summer while sitting in the garden, replied her son" (*Difficult Daughters* 30).
The context calls for a friendly protest.

(f) *cordiality in interrogation*—
"Arrey, Sen, where have you been? Join us . . ." (*English, August* 131).
" 'Arre baap,' she cries, 'where are you bringing me?' " (*Midnight's Children* 84)
The context requires the speaker to ask his companion warmly and in earnest.

(g) *objection/censure*—
"Are moshai, can I just say a word?" (*The Hungry Tide* 5)
"Arrey, I can't let a junior pay for me, hahn, bhai, how much?" (*English, August* 146)
"Arre, there is all the time in the world for sitting around, doing nothing?" (*Difficult Daughters* 6)
The situation demands that the speaker interrupt his companion, oppose or censure him.

4. Borrowed Words from *A Suitable Boy*

Indian literature today comprises fiction by writers with international reputation, living in India and abroad for whom

English is a second language. Vikram Seth's epic novel *A Suitable Boy*, set in the early 1950s, includes the years of Nehru, the passing of the zamindari abolition legislation and the first election of the post-independence era. In the novel, he has frequently referred to Hindi, Urdu, Bengali words, ranging over two hundred lexical items. These words with their lexical categorisation, inflectional selections and linguistic descriptions are discussed below :

1. *aai jao* "And when the bus was about to move, he would summon them with a battlecry of: 'aai jao bhaiyya, aai jao. Chalo ho!' " (645)
   aajao, "come on" is a single word in Hindi. From the sentence it is evident that it is a verb in second person singular. However, here it refers to a group of people. –*i* of *aai jao* is the emphasizer. The infinitive form of the verb is aajana.
2. *abba-jaan* "Abba-jaan, your munshi has arrived from Baitar. He wants to talk to you, . . ." (271)
   abba "father" is a kinship term in Urdu. The suffix –jaan is an honorific marker.
3. *achkan* "Ustad Majeed Khan was . . . seated on the stage in his long black achkan . . ." (298)
   achkan "a long full sleeved dress from neck to the knees, usually worn by males" is a noun. It is the name of a dress of Indian origin.
4. *adaab* "No wonder she loves doing adaab to anyone she sees." (80)
   adaab is a polite gesture of greeting people in Muslim culture. The word also carries an honorific sense.
5. *akhara* "It was sadhus from . . . akharas, . . . the striking part of the traditional procession that took place each year at the phul mela . . . ." (720)
   akhara "a large group from various sects or orders of sadhus" is a noun which combines with English inflectional marker "–s" to form a plural substantive.

6. *alokam* "Om alokam" (726)
aloka "light" is a noun in vocative case. The word is a part of a sutra in the narration.
7. *alaap* "After she had re-tuned it, the Ustad sang a few phrases of a slow alaap . . . ." (294)
alaap "the centre part of Hindustani Classical music" is a noun referred in the narration as a part of vocal classical music. It occurs with the English adjective 'slow'.
8. *alu* "Good. We have alu paratha today." (812)
alu paratha "a north Indian dish—a type of bread made by kneading together flour and potato or alu and fried in oil". It is a part of a compound noun in the sentence.
9. *anandam* ". . . Om anandam." (726)
ananda "happiness" is a noun in vocative case. This word is also a part of a sutra.
10. *angarkha* ". . . a small white kurta for Abbas, and a white angarkha for his elder brother." (277)
angarkha "a part of a dress for men" usually worn/kept over the shoulders is a noun.
11. *annakutam* "On five consecutive days around the end of October came Dhanteras, Hanuman Jayanti, Diwali, Annakutam and Bhai-duj." (1074)
These are all Hindu festivals which the author notes "some observed fervently, some luke warmly, some merely noted, some entirely ignored."
12. *arhar* ". . . hauling arhar stalks onto the roof of the house to dry for cooking fuel." (531)
arhar "a variety of pulses cultivated in summer" is a noun used as a specifier of stalks.
13. *arz* "Adaab arz, Chacha-jaan." (643)
arz "to show (respect)" is an Urdu verb in first person singular.
14. *baba* " 'What should I say, Baba?' said Amit." (419)
baba "father" is a kinship term in Bengali.
15. *bai* "The previous evening, when Maan had stopped by, Saeeda Bai had been entertaining . . . the Raja of Marh . . . ." (105)

bai "honorary title for women court singers" is a noun. It usually occurs after a female name.

16. *ballishtahs* "All the big people of Bombay, all the businessmen and ballishtahs stood up in court, ..." (519)
ballishtah "wealthy, powerful people" is a noun with the English plural marker '-s.'

17. *bania* ". . . this is the grasping attitude of the village shopkeeper, the bania who smiles . . . and grasps without any mercy—" (286)
bania "grocer" is a Hindi noun which combines with the definite article 'the' and the verb 'smile' in the sentence.

18. *baoji* " 'Yes Baoji,' said Maan, smiling." (6)
baoji "father" is a kinship term. The word also occurs in Manju Kapur's *Difficult Daughters* (9, 78, 220).

19. *basket-wallahs* "... he needed the shoes of the basket-wallahs, and they did not dare come to Misri Mandi these days." (243)
basket-wallah "hawkers carrying their goods in baskets" is a compound noun with the plural marker '-s.'

20. *begum* "Begum Abida Khan slowly stood up. She was dressed in a dark blue, almost black sari . . . . "(251)
begum "honorary address," wife of the Nawab, usually signifies aristocracy.

21. *behayaa* "Behayaa—besaram—how shameless can you get in the very face of your own death." (519)
behayaa, besaram "slang words" used as nouns in the text. Both are abusive words approximately meaning 'without any shame'. The word *bay-sharam* also occurs in Rohinton Mistry's *Such a Long Journey*.

22. *bhadralok* "But half the bhadralok in Calcutta want him as a match for their daughters, ..." (384)
bhadralok "elite people" is a noun, occurs with the English definite article 'the.' It is a Bengali compound word which in literal translation means gentlemen.

23. *bhairava* " 'Now which raag was I teaching you—Bhairava?' asked Ustad Majeed Khan." (292)
bhairava "name of a classical raag, usually sung in the morning" is a noun. Other classical raags mentioned in the text are Ramkeli, Pilu, Malkosh, Todi, Miya-ki-todi, Marwa.
24. *bhajan* "Kachheru hummed a bhajan to himself as he walked the bullocks out of the village." (532)
bhajan "a song of praise to god, especially one for use in a religious service" is a noun with the indefinite article 'a'.
25. *bhai-duj* "She did not even believe in Rakhi, insisting that the festival that truly sanctified the bond between brother and sister was Bhai-Duj." (722)
bhai-duj "a Hindu festival the day after Diwali," comes from 'bhai-ke liye dua' (seek blessings for the brother) is a festival between brothers and sisters.
26. *bhang* "He drank not just one but several glasses of thandai laced with bhang and was soon high as a kite." (73)
bhang "an intoxicant added in drinks during festivals". It is a noun in the sentence.
27. *bigha* "Well, no one is going to take away a single bigha of my land." (673)
bigha "unit for measuring land" (=3035 sq yds) is a noun with indefinite article 'a' and adjective 'single'.
28. *bilkul* "He held his ears . . . then lapsed into English: No, no, no, bilkul no!" (202)
bilkul "absolutely" is an adverb. The word spelt as bilkool occurs in Rohinton Mistry's *A Fine Balance* (308, 403, 423, 427).
29. *bulbul* " 'Oh, don't stop,' said Malati, nudging Lata gently. 'You have a nice voice. Like a bulbul.' " (23)
bulbul "name of a bird" is a noun. It has been used as a simile in the sentence.
30. *burqa* ". . . women shuffled along in anonymous burqas or bright saris . . . ." (89)

burqa "a long black dress from head to foot covering the face" is worn by some religious Muslim women. In the sentence it combines with the plural marker '–s' to form a plural noun.

31. *burri memsahib* " 'Burri Memsahib?' he called, knocking at the door of Mrs. Rupa Mehra's room." (33)
burri memsahib "elder lady" is a noun. The word burri signifies an elderly person (lady).
32. *chachi* " 'Abida Chachi?' 'Her telephone appears to be out of order, and I have just written her a note.' " (277)
chachi "aunty, father's brother's wife" is a term demarcating a specific relation or is a kinship term.
33. *chacha-jaan* "Very softly, her mother had said, 'Not Chacha-jaan. Abba-jaan.' " (643)
chacha-jaan "uncle", father's brother is a kinship term.
34. *chappatis* "Memsahib likes . . . to put some ghee every day on her chapatis . . . ." (67)
chapatti "a food item, type of thin bread usually circular in shape about 25 cm in diameter" is a noun with the plural suffix '-s.' The word also occurs in Rohinton Mistry's *A Fine Balance* (181).
35. *charpoy* " 'Probably not,' said Rasheed. 'Different owls, and probably not on a charpoy' ". (508)
charpoy "a four legged rectangular cot made of coir" is a noun with the indefinite article 'a'. The word also occurs in Manju Kapur's *Difficult Daughters* (153).
36. *chaupar game* "Normally he was a very polite man . . . but chaupar was chaupar, and it was almost impossible to stop playing once the game had begun." (94)
chaupar "a game played by throwing cowries on a board" is a noun without an article.
37. *chhote sahib* "Chhote Sahib—would be coming for breakfast immediately, and would Maan Sahib be pleased to go downstairs?" (102)
chhote sahib "younger master" is an adjective and a noun. Sahib is an honorific marker. Suffix '–e' after the main

word chota (younger) is the masculine marker for the adjective.

38. *chowk* "The police have a hard enough time controlling traffic in Chowk— . . . " (115)
chowk "crossing point" is a noun without an article.

39. *chunni* "Malati had had a lot to put up with: teasing, gossip, the pulling of the light chunni around her neck, ..." (29)
chunni "a piece of cloth of light fabric worn around the neck as a part of a dress by women" is a noun with the definite article 'the'. A synonym for the word, dupatta is also found in the narration.

40. *dada* " 'Yes Dada,' said Dipankar, who thought it best to be simply factual." (413)
dada "elder brother" is a noun. It is a kinship term in Bengali.

41. *daadi* "You can go, I don't care; if Daadi stays here I don't care two hoots." (310)
daadi "grandmother" is a kinship term. It is a noun in the sentence.

42. *dhakai* ". . . Dhakai saris with a white background and a pattern in the weave—or (still more elegant) a grey background with a white design . . ." (388)
Dhakai "a trade name derived from the Bangladesh capital Dhakka" is a noun with the derivative '-i' marker.

43. *dhakka lagaauu* "Are, du-char jane utari aauu. Dhakka lagaauu!" (645)
dhakka lagaauu "push" is a verb. In Hindi it has a compound structure of the substantive and the main verb. The word '*are*' is an interjection. It occurs nine times (spelt as 'arre') in Manju Kapur's *Difficult Daughters* and eight times (spelt as 'array') in Upamanyu Chatterjee's *English, August*. It is also found in the works of other authors.

44. *dharmasala* "Basil Cox will be coming within an hour and I don't want him to think I run a third-class dharmasala." (378)

dharmasala "a place for free boarding and lodging" is a noun with the indefinite article 'a'. The word is a compound noun.

45. *dhobi-ghat* "How much do you charge local people to take them all the way up to the Barsaat Mahal from near the dhobi-ghat?" (165)
dhobi-ghat "place for washing clothes" is a compound noun (dhobi 'washerman,' ghat 'place') with the definite article 'the'.
46. *dhoti-wallahs* "We're still an advancing society—as our dhoti-wallahs are fond of telling us." (1107)
dhoti "an Indian dress for males" *wallah* "a person (wearing a dhoti)," is a compound noun with the plural suffix '-s'. The word has a presuppositional meaning as well, 'pertaining to or connected with.'
47. *dupatta* "Don't twist the end of your dupatta, you'll crumple it." (160)
dupatta "a synonym for chunni" is a noun with the definite article 'the'.
48. *dushanda* "I'll give you some dushanda to cure it." (96)
dushanda "stuff used for clearing throats" is a collective noun without the plural marker.
49. *dussera-nights* ". . . but the nine nights of Dussera are still to come." (329)
Dussera "a Hindu festival usually celebrated for ten days in October or November," *dus*; ten, is a noun.
50. *ekadashi* "It is Ekadashi today." (36)
ekadashi "the eleventh day of the lunar fortnight, when widowed women fast in memory of their husbands" is a singular noun without an article.
51. *ek-dum* " 'Now have your milk.' To the ayah she said, 'Dudh lao. Ek dum!' " (59)
ek dum "immediately" is an adverb. The Bengali word for just now used contextually is *ekkhuni*. Ek-dum is not generally used.
52. *gajak* ". . . some in khaki, brought . . . gajak and ice-cream . . . ." (14)

gajak "a kind of sweet" is a noun without the plural marker.

53. *gulab-jamuns* ". . . some in khaki, brought . . . gulab-jamuns . . ." (14)
gulab-jamun "a sweet item" is a noun with the plural marker '-s'.

54. *gunda-gardi* "The whole of Bombay was outraged at this gunda-gardi, . . ." (518)
gunda-gardi "hooliganism" is a derived noun.

55. *hennaed hand* "She stretched her long neck lazily and pointed with the red-nail-polished finger of a delicately hennaed hand." (1342)
hennaed "designed with light brown juice of mehendi leaves" is an adjective in participial use.

56. *jatav caste* "These shoemakers, mainly members of the . . . jatav caste . . ." (99)
jatav "name of a caste (shoemakers)" is a noun with the definite article 'the'.

57. *jaymala* "They were supposed to come out from opposite ends of the house and meet here for the jaymala five minutes ago." (7)
jaymala "a ritual of the Hindu wedding" is a noun with the definite article 'the'.

58. *jeth purnima* "I don't believe it. That is why I never join the superstitious crowds who bathe on Jeth Purnima." (722)
jeth purnima "full moon of May/June." This according to the novel is a day of "the Phul Mela," the fair of flowers. It is a noun. *cf.* No. 5 above.

59. *jijaji* "And there is Kedarnath Tandon— who is Pran's jijaji—which makes him my jijaji's jijaji, but that is . . . a fairly close relation." (901)
jijaji "sister's husband" is a kinship term.

60. *karbala* "She contrasted the flippancy of Maan's remark with the terrible thirst of the heroes of Karbala — their tents burning behind them . . . ." (1052)
Karbala "name of a place of religious importance to Muslims" is a noun.

61. ***kababs*** "The first few guests were standing around sipping fruit juice . . . and nibbling kababs or nuts . . ." (78)
kabab "a sausage like food item without the casing usually made of chopped up meat or pulses" is a noun with the plural suffix '-s'.
62. ***karela*** "He was particularly fond of karela, the bitterest of all vegetables—" (177)
karela " a vegetable, bitter gourd" is a noun.
63. ***karma-yogi*** "He worked hard, but for the action, not for the fruits of the action. He was a true karma-yogi, . . ." (549)
karma-yogi "workaholic" is a compound noun with the indefinite article 'a' and is modified by 'true'.
64. ***kartik purnima*** "But for Brahmpur one festival, observed much more devotedly here than almost anywhere in India, that of Kartik Purnima . . ." (1080)
kartik purnima "full moon of October/November" is a compound noun.
65. ***karva chauth*** "It's Karva Chauth, and she can't eat from sunrise to moonrise: Or drink a drop of water." (1073)
Karva Chauth "the ninth day after Dussera when Hindu women fast for long life of their husbands" is a ritual day of the year. Karva is an adjective in Hindi, Chauth is a noun. Here it is a compound noun.
66. ***khaki turbaned*** "The khaki-turbaned watchman at the entrance appraised him for a moment . . . ." (101)
Khaki-turbaned "a person with a khaki coloured turban" an adjectival participle.
67. ***khan sahib*** " 'Khan sahib is very kind,' he said." (107)
khan sahib "an honorary form of address for Mr. Khan" is a noun.
68. ***Khandelwal devta*** "To them he was a living deity—Khandelwal devta ! . . . ." (916)
Khandelwal devta "Mr. Khandelwal who is looked upon as a deity" is a noun.
69. ***ki korchho*** " 'Ki korcho tumi, Dipankar? . . .' she began, and continued to upbraid him . . . ." (477)

ki korcho tumi "What are you doing." *Korcho* is a Bengali verb in second person singular.

70. *Kumbhkaran* " 'Asleep ! You are like Kumbhkaran,' said Bhaskar." (1045)
Kumbhkaran "a character of Ramayana" is a proper noun without the article.

71. *kurta* "Young Hashim looked down guiltily at his blue, embroidered kurta." (84)
kurta "Indian dress for males" is a noun.

72. *lakki kothi* ". . . she asked him whether he belonged to the Khannas . . . who lived in Lakki Kothi." (193)
lakki kothi "house, residence" is a compound noun.

73. *Lata bua* "Aparna, you must stay with your Mummy or with Lata Bua, otherwise you will get lost." (5)
bua "father's sister" is a kinship term.

74. *lathi-charge* "At one o'clock he was saying: 'Are you telling me that the lathi-charge was necessary? . . .' " (326)
lathi-charge "lathi 'stick" is a compound noun. According to Kachru, this is a hybrid compound word with one element from an Indian language.

75. *lobongolotikas* "The tea soon came in, together with a few delicious lobongolotikas . . . ." (476)
lobongolotika "is a Bengali sweet pastry, lobongo 'clove' " is a noun with the plural suffix '-s'.

76. *luchis* "Truly—but you must try the luchis." (400)
luchi "a Bengali fried food item circular in shape, made of flour about 10-12 cm in diameter" is a noun with the plural suffix '-s' and the definite article 'the'.

77. *mago* "Mago, your cook really saved my life yesterday." (398)
mago "Oh! Mother" is an interjection commonly found in Bengali.

78. *mahasabha* "To be fair, Sir, we could have given an equal amount to all these parties . . . to the Hindu Mahasabha . . . ." (963)
mahasabha "large gathering" is a Hindi noun.

79. *mali* "The small green garden was empty. The part-time mali had gone." (375)
mali "gardener" is a noun with the definite article 'the'.
80. *matthri* "First they had tea, and matthri, with a mango pickle that Mrs. Kapoor had herself prepared." (177)
matthri "crisp and flaky food item" is a noun.
81. *mausaji* " 'You are very good to Pushkar, Mausaji,' she said . . . ." (590)
mausaji "mother's sister's husband" is a kinship term.
82. *mihidana* "The journey passed peacefully and as planned, but I must admit I could not resist having some mihidana at Burdwan." (41)
mihidana "a Bengali sweet" is a noun which occurs after the quantifier 'some'.
83. *milaap* "I have to go to watch the Bharat Milaap, ..." (1052)
milaap "reunion, Bharat Milaap, an episode of Ramayana" is a noun.
84. *Misri Mandi* "As he entered the residential areas of Misri Mandi, the alleys became narrower and cooler . . . ." (91)
Misri Mandi "name of a locality" is a noun.
85. *morha* "He pulled up a morha and joined them." (1184)
morha "a stool made of cane in the shape of a hyperboloid of one sheet" is a noun with the indefinite article 'a'.
86. *mullah* ". . . I worked in a big shop, a very famous shop run by a mullah, . . ." (517)
mullah "a Muslim religious man" is a noun with the indefinite article 'a'.
87. *munshi* "How do you know the munshi won't want to take his spite out on her?" (667)
munshi "a man who takes care of an estate" is a common noun with the definite article 'the'.
88. *musafir* "Uth, jaag, musafir" (1224)
Uth jaag *musafir* "arise, awake, traveller" Musafir is a noun.
89. *naan* ". . . she too became involved in feeding them,

especially the younger one who was having trouble in tearing the naan." (270)
naan "a roasted type of bread usually buttered" is a noun with the definite article 'the'.

90. *Nanajaan* " 'You come too, Nana-jaan,' she insisted." (643)
Nanajaan "grandfather" is a kinship term.

91. *navratan* "But tell me, when the jeweller comes to your house next time will you be able to get an estimate? . . . especially for my navratan?" (246)
navratan "a necklace of nine precious stones" is a noun.

92. *Nawabzada* "And this is the first time that the Nawabzada has graced my poor lodging with his presence." (117)
Nawabzada "younger Nawab or king" is a noun with the definite article 'the'.

93. *neel darvaza* ". . . she asked him whether he belonged to the Khannas of Neel Darvaza . . ." (193)
Neel Darvaza "blue door, name of a dwelling" is a noun.

94. *nimbu-pani* "Just now you offered me nimbu pani." (33)
nimbu pani "water with lemon juice" is a compound noun.

95. *nivas* " . . . Dr. Seth should phone Prem Nivas immediately he returned." (1217)
nivas "house" is a noun in Hindi.

96. *pallu* "The pallu of her sari covered her head and a part of her face, . . ." (328)
pallu "an expanse of a part or an end of a sari" is a noun with the definite article 'the'. In Indian languages, it occurs without an article.

97. *pandits* " . . . the time that the pandits have given is coming up, and there is no sign of either the bride or groom !" (4)
pandit "a man who carries out ceremonial rituals" is a noun with the definite article 'the' and the plural suffix '-s'.

98. *pao* " 'Two-and-half annas per pao,' replied the vegetable seller." (364)

pao "a weight measuring unit about 250 gms" is a noun.

99. *parishad* " . . . we would have given an equal amount to all these parties . . . to Ram Rajya Parishad . . ." (963)
Ram Rajya parishad "council of the Kingdom of Rama" is a collective noun. In Hindi, the word usually occurs after a proper noun.

100. *Pasand Bagh* ". . . Saeeda Bai . . . lives in Pasand Bagh . . ." (91)
Pasand Bagh "literal translation 'pleasant meadow,' name of a residential quarter" is a proper noun.

101. *Pathan* "The girl was a Punjabi, and there were such enmity towards the Pathan . . . ." (520)
Pathan "a race of western India" is a noun with the definite article 'the'.

102. *patwari* "To make sure of this, . . . he went the next morning after breakfast to visit the village patwari, . . ." (540)
patwari "a government functionary who acts as record-keeper and accountant of village lands" is a noun with the definite article 'the'.

103. *peshawari* "Ustad Majeed Khan . . . took off his own peshawari chappals and entered the room." (291)
peshawari (chappals) "(slippers) made in Peshawar" is an adjective with the emphasis marker '-i'.

104. *phataphat* "'Give me money! Phataphat! Immediately!' he yelled." (199)
phataphat "quickly" is an adverb. In Hindi it is a reduplicated word.

105. *phirni* ". . . let's have some phirni afterwards." (361)
phirni "food item made out of milk, sugar and rice" is a noun with a quantifier, 'some'.

106. *phulkas* "Why is he taking so long making the phulkas?" (1041)
phulkas "food item, round baked flour pieces" is a noun with the definite article 'the' and the plural suffix '-s'.

107. *phupha* "Vilayat sahib never visits anyone, Phupha-jaan." (655)

phupha "father's sister's husband," is a kinship term.

108. *pitthu* "The barbaric children from rustic Rudhia ran around yelling as if they were playing pitthu on the farm." (14)
pitthu "a children's game" is a noun.

109. *purdah* ". . . Zainab . . . after her marriage, had disappeared into the world of purdah." (20)
purdah "curtain" is a noun with figurative use 'the world of purdah.'

110. *puris* ". . . those who were standing in the garden . . . replenished along with puris . . . six kinds of vegetables." (14)
puris "a food item, flat circular flour pieces fried in ghee" is a noun with the plural suffix '-s'.

111. *pyjama* "He was dressed simply and immaculately in a well-starched white kurta-pyjama." (109)
pyjama "loose trousers tied around the waist" is a noun with the indefinite article 'a'.

112. *Ramnavami* "Can't we do something about Ramnavami?" (178)
Ramnavami "a Hindu festival, the day before Dussera" is a noun.

113. *saakshi bhaava* "You must have the saakshi bhaava",--- (715)
saakshi bhaava "the feeling of witnessing" is a compound noun with the definite article 'the'.

114. *sadhikas* "One thing is a must to say, and that is we are all sadhikas, . . ." (727)
sadhikas "learners, feminine" is a noun with the plural marker '-s', which is absent in the Hindi version.

115. *salaam aleikum* " 'Wa aleikum salaam,' replied Maan." (525)
salaam aleikum "may God bless you" is an Urdu phrase used for greeting people.

116. *samdhin* "She was the samdhin—the 'co-mother-in-law'—of both of the others, the link in the chain." (177)

samdhin "relative through marriage" is a noun with the definite article 'the'.

117. *samiti* "We know of the overt and tacit support he gives that foul organization the Linga Rakshak Samiti, . . ." (253)
samiti "union, literal translation the union of the preservers of phallus" is a collective noun with the definite article 'the'.

118. *samosas* ". . . samosas . . . were consumed and replenished . . ." (14)
samosa "a food item, snack, cooked vegetables and spices in a tetrahedral flour case fried in ghee" is a noun with the plural suffix '-s'. The word also occurs in Rohinton Mistry's *Such a Long Journey*, (31).

119. *sangh* ". . . we would have given an equal amount . . . to the Bharatiya Jan Sangh, . . ." (963)
sangh "Indian peoples union" is a collective noun with the definite article 'the'.

120. *sankirtan* "You have now dancing and sermon and sankirtan and meditation." (715)
sankirtan "dancing and chanting in a rhythm the name of Lord Krishna" is a noun in Hindi.

121. *shahi darvaza* "She had never done so until she came to live with the Goyals of Shahi Darvaza." (239)
shahi darvaza "royal door" is a compound noun.

122. *shamiana* "Many of them folded their hands in respect before the photograph . . . on a table on the long white-sheeted platform at one end of the shamiana." (1221)
shamiana "a tent with a horizontal top" is a noun with the definite article 'the'.

123. *shantipuri dhotis* ". . . crisp Shantipuri dhotis edged with a fine line of gold and hand-creased to perfection . . ." (388)
shantipuri "a trade name for dresses, made at Shantipur" is an adjective with an emphasis marker '-i'.

124. *sharifa* "Mahesh Kapoor helped himself to a sharifa as well." (997)

sharifa "a fruit, pear" is a noun with the indefinite article 'a'.

125. *sharmaji* " 'I am sorry, Sharmaji,' said Mahesh Kapoor with some annoyance." (974)
Sharmaji "an honorary form of address for Mr. Sharma" is a noun.

126. *shehnai* "The high, reedy shehnai music burst into a pattern of speed and brilliance." (6)
shehnai "a blowing Indian musical instrument" is a noun with the definite article 'the'.

127. *sherbet-stand* "Firoz and Maan walked over to the sherbet-stand." (1052)
sherbet "a kind of drink" is a hybrid compound noun with two elements, one from Hindi. The word is found in Rohinton Mistry's *A Fine Balance* (7).

128. *sitam-zareef* "She's a real sitam-zareef, he thought to himself . . ." (126)
sitam-zareef "a tyrant" is a noun with the indefinite article 'a'.

129. *sollishtahs* ". . . she . . . said to the whole court—the High Court judge and all the high ballishtahs and sollishtahs and all—" (520)
sollishtahs "echoed word from ballishtahs, powerful people" is a plural noun with the marker '-s'.

130. *Shri Bhagvad Charit* "The crowds of pilgrims—many of whom were clutching copies of the Shri Bhagvad Charit, a yellow-covered edition of which was on sale here—" (724)
Shri Bhagvad Charit "a scripture of the Hindus" has the definite article.

131. *Sundar Kanda* ". . . at least let us . . . recite . . . the Sundar Kanda . . ." (178)
Sundar Kanda "one of the seven cantos of the Ramayana" is a noun with the definite article 'the'.

132. *taluqdar* ". . . this . . . vicious class of . . . taluqdars . . ." (282)
taluqdars "landlord" is a plural noun with the suffix '-s'.

133. *tarbuz ka bazaar* "In fact her mother Mohsina Bai settled in Tarbuz ka Bazaar, . . ." (91)
Tarbuz ka Bazaar "market for watermelons" is a name of a region or locality. It is a compound noun.

134. *tanpura* ". . . a man who strummed the tanpura —sat down and started tuning . . ." (79)
tanpura "a four stringed musical instrument" has the definite article 'the'.

135. *thandai* "He drank . . . several glasses of thandai . . ."(73)
thandai "a cold drink" is a noun without an article.

136. *thali* ". . . he washed . . . his grandsons' hands . . . and sat them down, each in front of a small thali . . ." (269)
thali "plate on which food is served" is a noun with the indefinite article 'a'.

137. *theka* "Do you know how to play a simple theka—"(296)
theka "a rhythmic beat on the tabla" is a noun with an indefinite article 'a'.

138. *thumri* ". . . a strain of thumri floated down the inner balcony and filtered through the door . . ." (336)
thumri "light Indian classical music/song" is a noun with the indefinite article 'a'.

139. *tissue-patola* "If he had been here, I could have worn the tissue-patola sari I wore for my own wedding . . . ." (3)
tissue-patola 'a kind of fabric' is an adjective.

140. *toba* "Saeeda Bai . . . ran screaming 'toba! toba!'to the harmonium, and quickly played a descending scale through two octaves." (865)
toba "Good heavens!" is an interjection.

141. *uth* "uth, jag, musafir" (1224)
uth "rise" is a verb in second person singular.

142. *vakil sahib* "Where is Vakil Sahib? Is he all right?" (739)
vakil "lawyer" is a noun without an article.

143. *vanaspati* ". . . artificial foodstuffs such as vanaspati ghee . . ." (1168)
vanaspati "vegetable oil" is a noun.

144. *zamindari* "The Governor also mentioned . . . that the enforcement of the Purva Pradesh Zamindari . . . is being delayed . . ." (1305)
zamindar "land owner" is a noun with the definite article 'the'. The marker '-i' signifies his real estate. (Purva Pradesh—literal translation of 'eastern province.')

Fourteen of these glossed words are listed in the Indian English Supplement of Hornby's *Oxford Advanced Learner's Dictionary of Current English*, 1996. These words are *achkan, amma, angarkha, bai, begum, bhadralok, bigha, burra, charpoy, dhakai, Nawab, paraatha, phluka*, and *puri.*

5. Words of Indian Origin from *Midnight's Children*

Salman Rushdie's *Midnight's Children*, published in 1981, is about an alternative history of India after independence which subverts the realistic conventions of historical writing. It is an autobiography of the fictional character Saleem Sinai. The following Indian words used in the novel are arranged in alphabetical order :

> *Aap* (16), *abba* (150), *akaswani* (166), *allah* (65), *ammi, amma* (164), *arre baap* (84), *ayah* (79), *baba* (200), *badmaash* (147), *bajra* (167), *betel-chewers* (39), *begum* (147), *bhagwani* (27), *biris* (216), *bulbul-e-din* (313), *calipha* (203), *chambeli* (155), *channa* (170), *chaprasi-hand* (33), *chavanni* (135), *choicest pasanda* (253), *chugha* (27), *chutney* (456), *cobra-walla* (86), *dharma-chakra* (122), *dhoti* (354), *duniya* (268), *gharrie* (32), *goondas* (35), *gullies* (35), *haddi-phaelwan* (241), *hakimi medicine* (67), *hartal* (33), *ikka* (32), *janata* (418), *janum* (96), *jowar* (167), *kali yuga* (200), *khansama* (38), *karmastan* (109), *khichri* (69), *khusro* (268), *kolis* (92), *korma* (41), *kulfi* (239), *lapis-lazuli* (91), *lassi* (152), *maha guru* (269), *maha lakshmi* (139),

mango kasaundy (155), *melee* (223), *morcha* (418), *mubarak* (113), *muslim muhallas* (69), *musk* (155), *nakkoo* (27), *nargisi kofta* (253), *nimbu-pani* (58), *pajamas* (17), *pakoras* (32, 170), *paan-shop* (39), *paan-wallah* (442), *parishad* (206), *pathan turbans* (354), *pista-ki-lauz* (239), *purdah* (34), *purushottam* (153), *ragi* (167), *rickshaw-wallahs* (52), *sahibs* (17), *sadhuji* (113), *samosas* (239), *samyukta* (191), *shaitan* (217), *shakti* (438), *shikara* (18), *takht-e-Sulaiman* (31), *takalluf* (288), *tu* (16), *vani* (268), *vakeel* (147).

6. Findings

It is interesting to note that among the parts of speech borrowed from the Indian languages, the majority belong to the nominal group. The nouns borrowed have lost their original gender differentiation and inflectional forms according to masculine and feminine differentiation and have combined with the English article rules. For instance, in *A Suitable Boy*, twenty-three of the nouns in the text have taken the definite article 'the' and thirteen of them, indefinite articles. Twenty-seven are without articles, eighteen of them have taken the English plural marker '-s' .There are also sixteen compound nouns and nine kinship terms. The verbs have been borrowed in both inflected and uninflected forms. There are eight verbs from Hindi, Urdu and Bengali. Adverbs such as *ek-dum*, *phataphat* and *bilkul* are found. Adjectives such as *hennaed-hand* are four in number. They are in uninflected forms. These borrowed adjectives have lost their original gender inflections according to the nouns, which they qualified and in the above case have taken the past suffix, '-ed' before the noun. Quantifier 'some' occurs with five nouns, mostly food items. Here it may be mentioned that in the sentence No. 75 above, the Bengali version does not require the plural suffix -s for the noun *lobongolotika*. There are two interjections from Bengali and one from Hindi. Nouns such as *gajak* occur without quantifier or plural marker.

In *Midnight's Children*, the borrowed words from Indian origin include nouns, adjectives, and addressive forms and compound nouns. There are fifty nouns of Indian origin, fourteen compound nouns and seven hybrid nouns. Besides these, there are two classifiers (aap, tu), one particle (arre baap), and three kinship terms. Compound nouns have two or more elements all of which are from Indian languages, such as nargisi kofta, dharma-chakra, etc. In hybrid nouns, there are two elements, one of which is from an Indian language and the other from English, for example, chaprasi-hand, paan-shop. Comparing the borrowed words from the two texts it is found that the number and range of words in *A Suitable Boy* is more than that of *Midnight's Children*. Nonetheless, there are some common words such as ***nimbu pani***, ***parishad***, ***purdah***, ***vakeel***, which occur in both the novels.

Chapter - 5

Functional Features

This chapter focuses on the functional features of Indian English. There is as yet no extensive study on the functional features of written or spoken Indian English. It is difficult to distinguish these features in terms of register-specificity and regional variations. *The Cambridge History of the English Language*, focused on some selected functional features of educated South Asian English. These include sentence structure, function items, tag questions, question formation, selection restrictions and reduplication. The outline of the chapter is as follows :

1. Repetition
2. Cliché
3. Indianisms
4. Findings

The chapter deals with the phenomenon of repetition found in Vikram Seth's *An Equal Music* and *A Suitable Boy*, the informality feature cliché found in the novels of Rohinton Mistry, Amitav Ghosh, Arundhati Roy and others, and the aspect of Indianisms in Rohinton Mistry's *A Fine Balance*.

1. Repetition

Repetition is the act or process or an instance of repeating words and phrases. In South Asian English with particular reference to the Indian subcontinent, it includes word classes as "*hot, hot coffee* (very hot coffee)," and "*small, small things* (many small things)." Repetition from conversational extracts are analysed in this section. Repetition in conversations is a common feature in Seth's two novels, *An Equal Music* and *A Suitable Boy*. *An Equal Music* is based on an intense and passionate world of classical music. Most of the main characters in the novel are English and it is a story of a professional violinist's love for a pianist whom he knew as a student in Vienna. The story moves through the cities of London, Vienna and Venice. *A Suitable Boy* is a novel of everyday life of several Indian families in the early fifties of the last century. Even though the two novels have been set up in different social and political backgrounds, the author has brought repetition as a distinct feature of Indian English. This is discussed in the following paragraphs.

Repetition from Vikram Seth's An Equal Music and A Suitable Boy

The study of conversation in discourse extracts of a novel is decisive in comprehending the complex interpersonal relationships of the characters. Repetition, conscious or unconscious in the speech of persons involved enables us to discern the intricate emotional build-up behind it. Data collected by scrutinising conversational passages from Vikram Seth's *An Equal Music* and *A Suitable Boy* were analysed to study repetition in both self-repetition, and allo-repetition, that is, when repetition is a joint work between speakers and their interlocutors. In the study, various types of repetitions are explored and then an attempt is made to classify them.

Self-repetition and allo-repetition serve a precise purpose, that is to say they focus on the intersecting forces acting between the characters. In a sense, when properly analysed, they might be said to succinctly replace passages several times their size. While some of the repetitions studied seem to indicate that they come as if out of a slot machine on the drop of a coin which may be a specific taunting or sarcastic or provocating remark, there are others which call for a much deeper analysis for comprehension. For instance, the following extracts from Vikram Seth's *An Equal Music* exemplify neglect and provocation as aspects of repetition :

(a) *"Oh Michael, you're such a bore, says Virginie." "You're always half asleep. Such a boring old git," she adds proudly.*
"Virginie, you're ODing on your English idioms. Yes, well, I've been thinking about that. I'm sixteen years older than you."
"So what? So what? Why do you always tell me you aren't in love with me?" (77)

(b) *" Michael," says Virginie. "I love you. You don't deserve it, but I do.*
And I don't want to see you tomorrow. I don't want to see you or talk to you until after you have played that stupid music. I told you about it."
"You didn't even believe it existed."
"I know. I know." (78)

The two responses by Virginie in (a) and by Michael in (b) are robotic. They are the result of continuous neglect and sheer provocation respectively.

There are a fairly large number of studies on repetition as one of the categories of communication strategies utilised by language learners. Yet a full-fledged study on the conversational pieces in fiction is very hard to locate. T. Ravichandran's "Ingestion, Digestion and Revulsion of Food and Culture in Anita Desai's *Fasting, Feasting*" analyses the linguistic strategies such as repetition and interruption by examining appropriate instances from Anita Desai's *Fasting, Feasting*. He found that the characters in the novel use repetition for reinforcing commands and enforcing submission from the subordinates. Repetition is also used for interruption and cross questioning and finally, phrases are repeated as if for casting a spell.

Repetition is utilised by EFL learners and by characters in Vikram Seth's *An Equal Music* for different purposes. While language learners utilise repetition to gain time when searching for the intended meaning of the interlocutor (Celce-Murcia, Dornyei and Thurnell, "Communicative Competence"), the characters in the novel repeat words and phrases to gain time and think of an answer. In the latter case emotions and feelings of various shades presumably are involved.

According to Tannen, repetition is "a resource by which conversationalists together create a discourse, a relationship and a world. It is the central linguistic meaning making compound strategy, a limitless resource for individual creativity and interpersonal development" ("Repetition in Conversation" 97). Tannen considers the repetition in a conversation under the categories of production, comprehension, connection and interaction ("Talking Voices" 48). The first three stand for creation of meaning in a conversation. The last one covers social goals which are: to get or to keep the floor, to show listenership, to provide back channel responses, to stall, to gear up to answer or to speak, to indicate humour and play, to savour or show appreciation of a good line or a good joke, persuasion, to link ideas and to ratify another's contributions. Instances of repetition vary ranging from repetition of exact words with similar rhythmic pattern to paraphrases and other variation such as changing the person, tenses or wording. Research publications on repetition strategies used by language learners have been summarised by Erlenawati Sawir. She writes :

> Pioneered by Tannen (1987), repetition in a conversation has been investigated by numerous other researchers (Murata 1995; Lyster 1998; Reiger 2003; Jensen & Vinther 2003). . . . Ferrara1994; Simpson 1994; Dumitrescu 1996; Perrin *et al.,* 2003 examine repetition in accordance with particular prosodic characteristics, namely intonations. ("Keeping Up with Native Speakers" 2)

K. Murata ("Repetitions") for example, conducts a cross-cultural study on repetitions, comparing repetition strategies used in NSE/NSE (native speaker of English), NSJ/NSJ (native speaker of Japanese), NSE/NSJ conversation. Murata has analysed the immediate repetitions of words and phrases in accordance with topic and subtopic boundaries based on intuition. Her study examines the following kinds of repetitions: interruption-oriented repetitions, solidarity repetitions, silence-avoidance repetitions, hesitation repetitions and reformulation repetitions. Further Sawir identifies seven functions of allo-repetition : repetitions that indicate participatory listenership, justify listenership, ensure correctness, request for confirmation, request for clarification, stall and indicate surprise. Allo-repetition (Tannen, "Repetition in Conversation") has been called differently by different investigators : two-party repetition (Murata, "Intrusive"), second-speaker repetition (Simpson, "Regularized Intonation").

For the present study, repetition of words and phrases occurring in forty eight conversational passages of *An Equal Music* were collected and scrutinised. Of these eighteen were selected for an indepth analysis. As evident from the data by Bandyopadhyay ("Repetition in the Conversational Extracts" 77-89), this section discusses in detail self-repetitions and allo-repetitions—these are classified further into eight categories. These are now elaborated below. The eight categories thus classified are: (1) as a rejoinder to provocation, (2) to avoid a direct answer, (3) to express disbelief or surprise, (4) to express appreciation, (5) to stall and to gain time to formulate a proper answer, (6) to get or to keep the floor, (7) to request clarification, and (8) to request confirmation.

(i) As a Rejoinder to Provocation

Repetition is found in the replies of characters when provoked or driven to anger presumably with a rising intonation, a grimace and a gesture. The repetition may be both a self-repetition and an allo-repetition as illustrated in the following seven extracts from *An Equal Music* and *A Suitable Boy*. The extracts are generally from *An Equal Music*. (Those taken from *A Suitable*

Boy are indicated by the abbreviation ASB). Extracts (c), (e), (f) and (g), are allo-repetitions and (h) and (i) are self-repetitions.

(c) *"What does he mean to you? Does he mean what I mean?"*
"Michael, stop this."
"What's happening to us?"
"Us ? Us ? What us ?" (327)

(d) *"Did you hear me? Mrs Rupa Mehra's high voice held an edge of anger.*
Yes (Lata).
Yes what ?
Yes, Ma, I heard you. I heard you. I heard you." (ASB 594)

In extract (c) Michael asks Julia to play with him again. He has a problem with the Toroni and maybe he needs Julia's help in solving it. Julia reacts almost with violence, says she will not be forced to play with anyone again. At this juncture Michael asks her point-blank, "What does he (James) mean to you ? Does he mean what I mean ?" Julia does not give a direct answer. Michael asks "What's happening to us ?" ("us" standing for Michael and Julia). Julia is infuriated at Michael's insinuation. To her James is now closer, more intimate. The repetition is accompanied by a rising intonation, a high tone and a grimace. It is used as a response to provocation. In the following extract (d), Lata repeats the words, "I heard you" twice. In this context, the repetition indicates her resolve not to accede to her mother's request, which is to say "sorry" immediately. It is a rude reply as a response to provocation.

(e) *"Please Mr. Glover, don't say these things. She was my friend. How can I give up what she has given me ?"*
"Given ? Given ? I am afraid that you are labouring under a misapprehension . . . " (363)

In the extract (e), Mr. Glover repeats the word 'given' with a rising intonation and a high tone of voice indicating his fury and annoyance at Michael's suggestion that his aunt had given him the violin.

(f) *"I knew. I knew !" exclaims Virginie. "And you lied to me. You lied and lied and said you weren't seeing anyone. And I believed you. How disgusting you are Michael. Let me speak to her."*
"Virginie, calm down — be reasonable —"
"Oh, I hate you English. Be reasonable, be reasonable. You have hearts like cement."
"Virginie, listen, I'm fond of you, but —"
"Fond. Fond. Put her on the phone. I'll tell her how fond you were of me." (165)

Michael's mind almost all the time keeps drifting back to Julia, so he is ill prepared for a call from Virginie and that at eleven thirty after he had a hard day and is quite in a hurry to get back to sleep. Virginie cannot sleep—Michael has not spoken to her in two weeks and thinks he is sleeping with someone, and wants to speak to her. Michael is unable to convince her that there is no one with him and in order to mollify her says he is fond of her. This only annoys Virginie. She stalls Michael and repeats the word "fond" with a rising intonation as a result of deep provocation. There is an identical use of repetition "be reasonable" by Virginie earlier in the passage due to provocation, only here it is accompanied by a rude reply.

(g) *"Oh, Piers," said Helen.*
"Oh Piers, oh Piers, oh Piers!" said Piers. "I've had enough. Let me out. I'll walk to the hotel." (85)

This altercation takes place between Helen and her brother Piers in a car on their way to the hotel. The other two passengers are Billy and Michael, the other members of the quartet. They were bothered by a sticky fan of the quartet, each having a different degree of resentment against him. In their bickering, Piers is annoyed at the other members of the quartet's attempt to pacify him. Provoked by his sister, he repeats "O Piers" twice in a rising tone accompanied by a grimace.

(h) *"Get a mobile phone, Billy," says Piers in a lazy-peremptory prefect-like tone.*
"Why ?" asks Billy. "Why should I ? Why should I get a mobile phone ? I'm not a pimp or a plumber." (10)

In this self-repetition Billy is annoyed at Pier's suggestion "Get a mobile phone, Billy" uttered in a lazy-peremptory prefect-like tone. He replies with a repeated "Why should I ?" probably with a rising intonation, high tone accompanied by a grimace and a gesture. His provocation also shows through in his rude hint that only pimps and plumbers use mobile phones.

(i) *"When are you playing next ?"*
"In a couple of weeks—at the Bösendorfer Saal.*"*
"And what ?"
"We're beginning with an early Beethoven—"
"Are you being deliberately unspecific ?"
"No Professor."
"Which ?"
"Opus 1 number 3. In C minor."
"Yes, yes, yes, yes," says Carl Käll, provoked by my mentioning the key. "Why ?"
"Why ?"
"Yes, why ?"
"Because our cellist loves it."
"Why ? Why ?" Carl looks almost demented.
"Because she finds it amazing and exciting." (17)

In the above passage Carl is in conversation with Michael. Here there are three repetitions. The first one "Yes, yes, yes, yes" by Carl Käll—a self-repetition indicates provocation. The provocation is caused by Michael's mentioning the key (C minor) which, it appears is unnecessary for Carl, an experienced music teacher. The third repetition by Carl "Why ? Why ?" —a self-repetition indicates Carl's anger at Michael's answer "Because our cellist loves it." That Carl was filled with anger and worry is apparent from the sentence: Carl looks almost demented. [For the second repetition see (v).]

(ii) To Avoid a Direct Answer

The characters in the novel, repeat words or phrases when they want to avoid a direct answer to an inconvenient question and maybe also to change the topic. The rejoinder is sharp, hurried and possibly accompanied by a gesture and is found in the self-repetition category.

(j) *"We are asked to record the 'Art of Fugue'."*
"The 'Art of Fugue'? All of it?"
" Yes. By Stratus."
"Michael, that's absolutely amazing." Julia's face lights up with pleasure, with happiness at the thought—and surely for me.
"Yes, isn't it?" I say. "You used to play bits of it. Do you still ?"
"Sometimes. Not often."
"I've got the music. And there's an upright in the next room."
"Oh, no, no—I can't, I can't." She protests almost violently, as if warding off some terror (117-118)

Julia repeats the words "Oh, no, no— I can't, I can't" to register a protest and to ward off an implied uncompliable request from Michael to play Stratus' "Art of Fugue." "I have got the music. And there is an upright in the next room." Julia's refusal to play Stratus' "Art of Fugue" shows her disinclination to revive the past associations. Here the repetition indicates avoidance of recalling past memories.

(k) *"Eight thirty. Michael, I can't just drop Luke at school and then come and see you. I can't. It would be too—I don't know—too dismal."*
"Why not ? What have we done ?"
Julia shakes her head. "Nothing. Nothing. And I don't want anything . . . ." (119)

Michael earnestly requests Julia to come to him in the morning. For Julia it would be too difficult. Michael thinks Julia is trying to avoid him (dodge him) and so asks "Why not ? What have we done ?" Julia's use of the word 'nothing' twice indicates that she wants to conceal her hurt feelings and avoid a direct answer. She is in a hurry to change the topic "I don't want anything."

(iii) To Express Disbelief

Repetitions presumably with a rising intonation and a high tone of voice occur in the speech of the characters to indicate disbelief or surprise is illustrated in self-repetition and allo-repetition in the following examples. There is allo-repetition in (l) and (m) and self-repetition in (n).

(l) *"That's marvellous, Helen," I say. "Now eat up. This calls for a celebratory glass of mineral water."*
"Water?" says Helen, blinking. "Water ? Is that all your enthusiasm amounts to ?"
"Water," I say firmly, looking at my watch. "And perhaps a coffee if we've still got time."
"Wine," says Helen. "Wine. Without life, wine isn't worth living." (161)

(m) *"After a pause, Netaji said, You must have a lot of contacts.*
Contacts ?
Yes contacts, contacts, you know what I mean.
But—
You should use your contacts to help us, said Netaji bluntly."
(ASB 617)

In extract (l), besides the slip of the tongue "Without life, wine isn't worth living" Helen expresses disbelief, surprise at Michael's mentioning of the fact that he would prefer a glass of mineral water. Helen had expected wine. She repeats the word "water" with a high tone, facial expression and gesticulation. In extract (m), Maan did not expect that Netaji would talk about contacts to him. His repetition expresses disbelief while Netaji's repetition indicates confirmation.

(n) *"You know that Beethoven string quintet you told me about? I've got hold of the music, and we'll be playing it through the day after tomorrow. I want to have a good look at it first."*
"Oh, but that's wonderful, Michael. Why don't I join you to play it ?"
"Now, Virginie, wait a second—"
"No, listen. You play the second viola since you always say you miss the chance to play the viola, and I will play the second violin."
"No, no, no, no—I cry, warding off the thought like a swarm of bees." (77)

This is a self-repetition. The conversation is between Virginie and Michael. Here Michael's repetition of the word 'no' three times indicates his vehement opposition to Virginie's suggestion that he will play the second viola and she will play the second violin in the concert. Here the repetition function indicates Michael's doubt or disbelief that Virginie will play the second violin in the concert befittingly.

(iv) To Express Appreciation

Self-repetitions, maybe with a rising tone accompanied by facial expressions and gestures are used by characters in the novel to express appreciation of a good musical performance, ecstasy of delight as in :

(o) *We open the door and Erica Cowan marches in with her arms spread in welcoming rapture. She is followed by twenty or thirty people.*
"Marvellous, marvellous, marvellous, mwah, mwah, mwah!" goes Erica dispensing lateral kisses." (90)

Erica's self-repetition of the adjective (marvellous) stands for her appreciation of the success of the programme in which Michael and the other members of the quartet had played the first contrapunctus of Bach's "Art of Fugue". She repeats "marvellous" twice in a rising tone accompanied by gesticulations and goes dispensing lateral kisses.

(p) *"Welcome back to London, welcome, welcome, welcome. I hear it was an enormous success," says Erica. "Congratulations, congratulations, well done ! Lothar was raving about it."*
"Lothar wasn't there," I reply, moving the receiver a bit farther away from my ear.
"I know," says Erica slightly chastened. "He was in Strasbourg—sorry Salzburg—silly me !"
"Lunch at the Sugar Club, Erica ?"
"No, no, no, just a slip. I hope Piers didn't mind . . . I wish I had been there to hold all your little hands, especially during that interval, but there it is, there it is. Next time !"
"Who told you about that ?"
"About what ?"
"The interval."
"No one, no one, I just picked it up from here and there . . ."
(297)

Erica conveys her delight and pleasure in a telephonic conversation with Michael by saying "welcome" thrice and "congratulations" twice. The repetitions here are self-repetitions and express appreciation. But she lies when she says "Lother was raving about it." Her slip of the tongue "He was in Strasbourg—sorry Salzburg" is a direct consequence of her having been chastened by Michael's reply. Michael suggests the slip could have been due to drinks "Lunch at the Sugar Club, Erica ?" Erica repeats the word 'no' three times to negate his suggestion. Next Erica says that she would have liked to be there and hold Michael's hands during that interval and repeats the phrase 'there it is' meaning thereby that it is all over and there is no point in repenting over it now. This refers to an incident, which took place during the interval recounted earlier (241) when Michael was indisposed and Julia pressed his hands to encourage him to go on to the stage and play. Erica repeats the phrase 'no one' in answer to Michael's query "Who told you about that ?" to avoid a direct answer and apparently to conceal the name of the informant.

(v) To Stall and to Gain Time to Formulate a Proper Answer

Some repetitions are found to function as stalling, that is to gain time to formulate an answer. The interlocutor's question may want thinking out, hence the need to stall for time for an appropriate answer. It is an allo-repetition.

(i) *"When are you playing next ?"*
"In a couple of weeks at the Bösendorfer Saal.*"*
"And what ?"
"We're beginning with an early Beethoven—"
"Are you being deliberately unspecific ?"
"No Professor."
"Which ?"
"Opus 1 number 3. In C minor."
"Yes, yes, yes, yes," says Carl Käll, provoked by my mentioning the key. "Why ?"
"Why ?"
"Yes, why ?"

"Because our cellist loves it."
"Why ? Why ?" Carl looks almost demented.
"Because she finds it amazing and exciting." (17)

The second repetition "Why" is an allo-repetition. Here Michael repeats "Why" with a falling intonation to bide time to think of an answer "Because our cellist loves it." [The first and the third repetitions have been discussed in (i)]

(vi) To Get or to Keep the Floor

Repetition presumably with a rising intonation and high tone accompanied by facial expression and gesture is used by Virginie in the example below in her attempt to get or to keep the floor from Michael who was trying to have the upper hand "I'm sixteen years older than you."

(a) *"Oh Michael, you're such a bore," says Virginie. "You're always half asleep. Such a boring old git," she adds proudly. "Virginie, you are ODing on your English idioms. Yes, well, I've been thinking about that. I'm sixteen years older than you."*
"So what ? So what ? Why do you always tell me you aren't in love with me ?"
"I didn't say that." (77)

Virginie had a number of grievances against Michael. She is found to argue with him. Her calling him names "such a bore, always half asleep, such a boring git" incites his resentment "I'm sixteen years older than you." Virginie repeats the question "So what ?" to get or to keep the floor.

(vii) To Request Clarification

In the passage below both the repetitions "By sea?" —Julia's; "No?" — Michael's for clarification signify that there is a lack of mutual understanding or that the characters are incapable of realising each other's feelings or points of view. Both are allo-repetitions. Julia repeats the phrase "By sea?" with a rising intonation to indicate her disbelief, unexpectedness, surprise.

(q) *"So this, then, is the Grand Canal."*
"This, then is it," says Julia, with a small smile.
"Should we have come by sea ?"
"By sea ?"
"By sea at sunset ?"
"No."
"No ?"
"No."
I grow quiet. (257)

(viii) To Request Confirmation

Repetition with a rising tone is used as a request for confirmation when the person wants his interlocutor to repeat a word or phrase or his whole message. The following allo-repetitions function to request confirmation.

(r) *"I had a lovely chat with Ysobel this morning—but let's talk about all this tomorrow at two."*
"Not two. Five."
"Five?"
"Five. Write it down." (105-106)

(s) *"You want to be close to me, to understand me, don't you ? (Saeeda Bai)*
Yes, yes of course.
Why, Dagh Sahib ?
Why ? Asked Maan incredulously.
Why ? persisted Saeeda Bai.
Because I love you." (ASB 354)

The conversation between Erica and Michael in extract (r) shows repetition of the word "Five?" by Erica probably with a rising tone requesting confirmation of the meeting time. Michael confirms "Five. Write it down". In extract (s), Saeeda Bai has a hunch that Dagh Sahib loves her but she wants him to say it and so repeats the question "why" for confirmation.

It is not always easy to specify the exact function of a particular repetition. Some repetitions need additional clues for a proper interpretation. In the literature on the EFL learner's repetition strategies it was found that the interpretation of repetition in a conversation depends on diverse factors : the situation, the relationship between and the mood of the interlocutors, prosodic features such as tone (Perrin *et al.*, "Pragmatic Functions"), intonation pattern (Simpson, "Repetition in Discourse"), and other paralinguistic features such as gesture and facial expression (Bolinger, "Intonation and Its Use"; Selting, "Prosody as an Activity-Type"; Perrin, *et al.*, "Pragmatic Functions"). Sawir also emphasises the importance of intonation pattern in interpreting the function of allo-repetition.

The repetitions of the characters in the novel (AEM) indicate that though some of them were found in the EFL learners repetition strategy, their import and nature differ to a considerable extent. Thus for instance, repetition to avoid a direct answer also includes a conscious attempt to hide hurt or real feelings. Again disbelief or surprise causing repetition is a much more complex range of feeling.

The data discussed in the section enable us to draw the following inferences :

- The self-repetitions and allo-repetitions are almost equal in number (8 and 10 respectively). From the table, it becomes clear that SR and AR occur in five categories each, though the categories are different. Only in two, (1) as a rejoinder to provocation, and (2) to express disbelief or surprise, both SR and AR are present.
- The phenomena of repetition as found in the data discussed above in responses are associated with some clusters of verbs of the same lexico-semantic group like :
  (a) annoy, irritate, tease

(b) relish, appreciate, enjoy, savour
(c) distrust, disbelieve, doubt

- From the novel *A Suitable Boy* repetitions for the categories as a rejoinder to provocation, to express disbelief, and to request conformation are found. All of them are allo-repetitions.

The analysis is presented in a tabular form in Table 5.1. The rows represent the eight functions: (1) as a rejoinder to provocation, (2) to avoid a direct answer, (3) to express disbelief, (4) to express appreciation, (5) to stall and to gain time, to formulate a proper answer, (6) to get or to keep the floor, (7) to request clarification, and (8) to request confirmation.

Table 5.1

Categories	*SR*	*AR*	*Rising intonation*	*Falling intonation*	*High Tone*	*Low Tone*	*Facial Expression*	*Gesture*
1. Provocation	+	+	+	-	+	-	+	+
2. To avoid a direct answer	+	-	+	-	+	-	-	+
3. To express disbelief	+	+	+	-	+	-	+	+
4. To express appreciation	+	-	+	-	+	-	+	+
5. To stall and to gain time, to formulate a proper answer	-	+	-	+	-	+	-	-
6. To get or to keep the floor	+	-	+	-	-	+	-	+
7. To request clarification	-	+	+	-	-	+	-	-
8. To request confirmation	-	+	-	+	-	+	-	+

The columns show the distribution of the features: self-repetition (SR), allo-repetition (AR), prosodic features— rising intonation, falling intonation, high tone, low tone and paralinguistic features—facial expression and gesture.

2. Cliché in Indian English Fiction

Indian writers in English sometimes do not exert themselves to find an original phrase. Instead they prefer to do with some prefabricated or conventional overused "pat" expression (Alam, "The Cliché and Indian English Fiction" 51). From the earlier fictional writings of Indian English, one comes across Raja Rao's clichés like "to tell you the truth" (*Kanthapura* 20). Cliché-like expressions such as "wonder of all wonders" occur in Mulk Raj Anand's fiction (*Coolie* 31). As pointed out by Alam (51, 52) R. K. Narayan's cliché expressions are a distinct feature of his simple style. Among others there are "odds and ends" (*Swami and Friends* 32; *The Vendor of Sweets* 25), and "out of sight out of mind" (*The Bachelor of Arts* 144). The term cliché is a phrase, or an idea that has been overused. In this section, clichés from Indian English fiction are classified into the following six broad types.

(i) Simile

Many similes found in Indian English are "mere clichés with very little left in them" (Vallins, *The Best English* 44):

> ". . . he had been like a *loving brother.*" (*SALJ* 14)
> "He was like a *little magician.*" (*TGOST* 74)
> "The sound of a thousand voices spread over the frozen traffic like a *noise umbrella.*" (*TGOST* 65)

(ii) Multi-Word Expressions : Literal Translations from Indian Languages

> " . . . *my right hand I will cut off and give you* if your biceps don't increase by one inch in six months." (*SALJ* 42)
> "I can eat *walking-walking.*" (*SALJ* 72)

This is also found in *A Suitable Boy* as in :

"'Forgot !' said Mrs. Rupa Mehra. 'Forgot. *You will forget your name* next.'" (*ASB* 1111)

(iii) The Conventional Verb Phrase

"... that's how the dark forces worked, ... striking when *least expected.*" (*SALJ* 260)
"What's happened *has happened.*" (*SALJ* 268)

(iv) Adjective + Noun Combinations

"*Idiotic-lunatic* talk is starting again." (*SALJ* 68)
"Every bloody peon or a *two-paisa* clerk is a B.A. these days." (*SALJ* 69)

(v) Circumlocution

An appropriate example is from Amitav Ghosh's *The Shadow Lines*, (henceforth referred to as *TSL*)."I would look in my (looking) glass and there he would be, growing, always *a head taller* than me, ..." (i.e., 'elder') (*TSL* 51), and
"... it was to those slopes ... she pointed when she told me that if I didn't study hard *I would end up over there*, ..." (i.e., 'in poverty') (*TSL* 134).

(vi) Vogue Expressions

"... *don't repeat your nonsense* about the bookcase." (*SALJ* 111)
"... the Bonesetter's methods are amazing. I am a *living witness*." (*SALJ* 60)
"I don't want any of your *khikhi-khaakhaa*." (*SALJ* 240)

Thus writers of Indian English in the past and at present have been accustomed to use these sets of expressions or clichés without introducing any fresh flavour into them. The presence of clichés reminds one that the writers are mostly bilingual.

These are in many cases obstacles for the native speakers of English. Excessive use of cliché and hackneyed phrases is normal and practised widely by writers of English in India.

The point to be added here is that in some authors like Arundhati Roy, there are original phrases instead of hackneyed ones. She has used words and phrases in an imaginative way to describe two things in order to extract their uncanny similarity, which in turn has made the description powerful. Apart from the metaphors and similes from the novel *The God of Small Things*, there are also a couple of instances such as, "a mango hair between the molars" (32), "old roses on a breeze" (55), "Pickle Baron dreams" (57), "the rhythm of a bus bhajan" (61), "car-shaped herbivore" (71), "bright feverbutton eyes" (109), "the dinner-smelling sea" (123) and "kind-school teacher voice" (173). Other cliché-like expressions are " . . . her thin grey hair plaited into a rat's tail" (256), "A lucky leaf that wasn't lucky enough" (73), "the WHAT snapped, barked, spat out" (107), " . . . wagged her rose at him" (142). Some expressions like "a cold moth lifted its legs," "Little man. He lived in a caravan" have been used again and again. One of the possible reasons may be that the narration is made from children's point of view and thus simplicity is a distinct characteristic feature.

Amitav Ghosh in his novel *The Shadow Lines* has used several well-worn clichés. Some of which are "move into his orbit" (5), "the only weapon people like us had was our brains" (134), "Don't talk . . . as though I were a secretary in your office" (151), "My father had laughed so much, he was hiccupping" (168), "He knew: he read books"(214). A possible explanation why Amitav Ghosh has used commonplace clichés is that most of these, used by the Indian characters in the novel are found in Bengali, and parts of the story are located in Kolkata and Bangladesh.

3. Indianisms

English as a second language in India has incorporated the social and cultural terms, expressions and norms from the vernacular first languages. These features unique to the Indian sub-continent which would otherwise remain restricted to the first language users of the country, have surfaced through Indian English fiction to the English literary world. According to V. K. Gokak: "By 'Indianism' is generally meant a word, phrase, idiom, expression or point of syntactical usage which is not part of current English or American usage and involves a shade of meaning or usage which is peculiarly Indian or is reminiscent of the lexis, idiom, phrase or syntax current in one of the modern Indian languages" ("A Brief Note" 25). The terms and expressions or common "Indianisms" are often difficult to interpret for the western readers. These features from Rohinton Mistry's *A Fine Balance* are considered in the following section.

Indianisms in Rohinton Mistry's A Fine Balance

A Fine Balance by Rohinton Mistry portrays the image of India during the Emergency, containing within it limitations of joy and disgust. In the novel there are sixteen episodes which begin with a prologue in 1975 and ends with an epilogue in 1984. In some portions of the novel, the language appears to be "Indlish" (the speech variety where Indian words are found within English constructions). This section focuses on the linguistic features of Indian English of the novel. The language of the novel is spoken by Indian characters in Indian social contexts. The narration, similar to most Indian English novels, represents non-linearity. The analysis as pointed out in Bandyopadhyay, "Indianisms" is based on Braj B. Kachru, Ramesh Mohan, and S.K. Verma's discussions on Indian English.

The language of the novel is markedly distinct in its Indianness. The sociological and cultural factors in the use of English as second language are examined in detail. Indian English writers such as Amitav Ghosh, Upamanyu Chatterjee, Vikram Seth and others are generally bilinguals. The English of the novel is a result of the interaction of two or more forms of language being in contact with each other. According to Kachru ("The Indianness in Indian English"), Indian English is intelligible not only to other Indians across the subcontinent but also to educated native speakers of English. The constructions from the novel are discussed in terms of mutual intelligibility (Hockett, *Course in Modern Linguistics* 323), acceptability, and unacceptability by other Indians. Mistry makes use of various forms of ambiguous speech and is favourably particular about using puns. His writing has contextual components of Indianness which can be understood if one takes into account the linguistic and cultural setting of India. Scholars have identified the linguistic factors of Indian English. The factors identified in the novel are (1) transfer of context, (2) transfer of L1 (an Indian language) meanings to L2, (3) transfer of form-context component, (4) grammatical deviations, (5) Indian expressions and terms, and (6) Hybrid Indianism.

(i) Transfer of Context

Mistry has transferred the cultural patterns which are absent in cultures where English is used as a native language. The cultural patterns which are found in the novel, under such transfer are : the caste system, social attitudes, social and religious taboos, superstitions, notions of superiority and inferiority as in the following :

(a) "For death, they came to me—for saros—nu—paatru, for afargan, baaj, farosky. But for a happy occasion, for wedding ashirvaad, I am not wanted." (37)
The above are Parsi religious terms, the exact meaning of these terms have been kept unexplained in the novel.

(b) " . . . wash off those hair clippings before you bring misfortune upon us !" (24)
This is a superstitious convention found among Parsi social communities.

(c) "... their family belonged to the chamaar caste of tanners and leather-workers." (95)
A caste is one of the fixed social classes in India, chamaar refers to a low caste.

(d) "On that happy morning they garlanded Xerxes with roses and lilies, and made a large red teelo on his forehead." (29)

It is the social custom of celebrating birthdays amongst the Parsi community. A red "teelo" is a long red mark put vertically along the forehead.

(ii) Transfer of L1 Meanings to L2 Items

The process may be restricted at the lexical level or it may include units like sentence, clause, phrase, collocation or compound word. For the lexical transfer Kachru has suggested that the meaning of an item of an Indian language is sometimes transferred to an item of English. An example from Kachru is the use of "flower-bed" in the sense of a nuptial bed by B. Bhattacharya, who has transferred the Bengali word *phul shojja* to a lexical item of English. The following sentences from the novel *A Fine Balance* indicate transfer of L1 meanings to L2 :

(a) "Omprakash broke the silence by pointing out a watermelon sherbet stand." (7)
Here the transfer of meaning watermelon sherbet stand has resulted in the extension of register range of an item of L1. In English, "stand" is restricted to the register of flower stand. "Sherbet stand" is formed in Indian English due to the extension of the register-range of the item.

(b) "Nusswan will jump over the moon." (23)
The phrase "jump over the moon" is an idiom, which refers to severe criticism or finding fault with someone.

(c) "... he yelled at the ones settled serenely in lotus position." (136)

Lotus position is a sitting posture with folded legs and erect spine. The legs are folded in a special way one above the other. This is an Indian way of sitting commonly known as *padmasana* in yoga.

(d) " . . . shall I do some more chumpee for your feet ?" (141)

Chumpee is pressing or massaging the feet, an Indian method used to enhance proper blood circulation. Here an Indian concept has been transferred to Indian English.

(iii) Transfer of Form-Context Component

These are the contextual units which are Indian and not found in the native varieties of the English language. As Kachru observes :

> Such contexts may be called Indian contexts as opposed to purely English or American context. . . . In Indian languages, (which Indian English writers use as their L1's), there are specific formal elements which function in such Indian contexts, and . . . are transferred to Indian English. These . . . [are] Indianisms. ("Indianness in Indian English" 399)

At the lexical level these Indianisms are found in collocational deviation. In the novel, Indianism of speech functions such as abuses, curses, greetings, blessings, flattery are found. Some instances from AFB are mentioned below :

(a) *Curses:* "Shameless woman ! What a loose mouth ! Such blasphemy." (52)

"Arrey saala go! Nobody is forcing you to buy!" (398)

"Saala shameless budmass ! Torturing innocent children !" (362)

"Saala gandoo ! Save it for the mohallas of the heartless rich." (362)
"Worse than Ravan!" (362)

(b) *Greetings:* "A little sahibji-salaam was enough . . . ." (55)
"Sahibji- salaam" is a social custom of greeting people. "-ji" honorific is a double assertion.

(c) *Flattery:* "Aray, hero–ka–batcha !" (347)
Here the author has used the Hindi suffix "ka–batcha" with the word "hero," to give its meaning "son of a hero". It is a common idiom of Indian languages, being incorporated into Indian English which is used to address/taunt people who try to act smart in a particular situation.

(d) *Abuses :* "How much nonsense you boys are talking, said Ishvar. Been smoking ganja or what ?" (311)
In Indian languages, the notion of talking nonsense as a result of consumption of 'ganja' (opium) or drugs is widespread. In the context, Ishvar is in disagreement with the remarks made earlier and reviles the boys.
"Hey ? You want free bus ride ? Your father's Divali or what ?" (267)
Divali, the Indian festival is usually seen as a celebration time when people spend money for fun and enjoyment. The phrase 'father's Divali' has been used in a negative sense to ridicule, to deride in the context.

(iv) Grammatical Deviations

In incorporating Indianisms, there is transfer of lexical and grammatical structure which results in deviations from the native English. The grammatical deviations include the use of present continuous forms in place of other tenses such as :

(a) " 'You are asking the wrong people,' said Ishvar." (6)
Here the author has used "are asking" (present

continuous) instead of "have asked" (present perfect). *cf.* Hindi: *puch rehe ho*. In most Indian languages, present continuous tense is used for expressing this sense.

(b) "See, simply you were panicking . . . " (6)
In the above example, "were panicking" is found in place of panicked. *cf.* Hindi *taras rahe ho*. Similar to example (a) the present continuous form, widely used in Indian languages, has been incorporated into Indian English.

(c) "Today I'm just going to meet her . . . " (6)
In the construction "just going" has replaced I'll go and meet her. *cf.* Hindi *sirf ja raha hoon*. "Just" is the translation of Hindi *sirf*, which is also interpreted as now. Thus an equivalent form of *sirf* is established in Indian English. The construction "I was just going to tell it, . . ." from Vikram Chandra (*Red Earth and Pouring Rain*, 26) also gives the same semantic interpretation of the adverb of time. It is however difficult to say whether on the part of an Indian English writer, the attempt to establish equivalence is conscious or unconscious. Some writers like Salman Rushdie in *Midnight's Children* and Amitav Ghosh in *The Hungry Tide* have deliberately used equivalence in their language.

(d) "Maneck, I really think you should do what your mummy is requesting." (493)
In this example, "is requesting" (present continuous) occurs instead of "has requested" (past perfect). *cf.* Hindi *bata* (= say, in place of request) *rahe hai*.

(e) "Not at all. I am looking after the flat, don't worry." (552)
In this sentence, "am looking after" occurs for "will take care." *cf.* Hindi *dekh bhal kar raha hoon*. The construction is found in Indian English due to shift or adaptation (Hindi *dekh* = English 'looking'). But here the connotation of Hindi *dekh bhal karna* is "to take care of." In such shift equivalents, connotative elements are not established. An Indianism occurring due to shift

is the adaptation of an underlying item of an Indian language which can be identified as its source. The source of a shift is a fixed collocation of an Indian language.

(f) "Actually speaking, I didn't see anything." (570)

Here the collocation "actually speaking" is transferred from an Indian language to Indian English. *cf.* Hindi *asli baat*. According to Kachru, "a creative writer may mainly be interested in "building up" a native contextual unit in L2, and, for that, translation from L1 may be used as a language device" ("The Indianness" 402).

In this transfer of item of an Indian language, the Indian English writer, who is also a bilingual may have done it deliberately to reveal the speaker's linguistic coordinates (which may include besides his L1, his country, social class, etc.). It should be added here that the speaker's location in the multidimensional linguistic space is possible only with his pronunciation and intonation details, which are not provided by the written literature.

(g) "Daddy was fond of dramatics. But now you are doing just that." (392)

The use of "are doing" in the construction is due to a translation from an Indian language, *cf.* Hindi *kar rahe ho*. Here the author has attempted to translate an item of Indianism in the same lexical category as in Indian English.

(h) "All the traffic is stopped." (54)

The author has used the auxiliary "is" in place of "has". The copula is the reflection of the present tense form found in similar situations in Indian languages.

In the novel, the author has used instantaneous present in situations other than the prescribed ones. From the instances that are given above, it is obvious that the larger (in comparison with native English) range of the present continuous tense of Indian languages has gradually become one of the grammatical features of Indian English.

(v) Indian Expressions and Terms

A number of Indian expressions and terms occur in the novel. These terms are originally from Indian languages and they are found in Indian English through the writings of the bilingual authors who write in Indian English. Examples of the deviations from the native language incorporated into English are the following :

(1) "*Paan* we don't chew only, said Ishvar. But sometimes we like to smoke a *beedi*." (9)
From the above sentence, it is evident that *paan* and *beedi* are items for chewing and smoking respectively. Other than this, for the non-native speaker, the identities of the items are not apparent from the context.

(2) "The knots ranged in size from microscopic to a bulky *samosa*." (31)
Samosa is a fried food item, which is usually tetrahedral in shape, where spicy potatoes are stuffed inside a kneaded flour casing. The word is used here to refer to the increase in the size of the knot.

(3) "Or we can hire a matchmaker. I hear that Mrs. Ginwalla has the best track record for successful *kaaj*." (51)
Kaaj is an Indian word. In Hindi, it means work. The work here specifically refers to marriage alliance.

(4) "Shaking his head and muttering about the stupidity of these *achhoot jatis*, . . . " (102)
In Indian society, *achhoot jatis* refers to the class of people who are known as untouchables. This caste distinction, unique and age-old for the Indian society has been embodied in the novel through Indian English.

(5) "While Dukhi and the child slept, she crept out of the

hut with a small brass *haandi*, . . ." (97)
"Flames licked the black bottom of a huge *karai* full of boiling oil." (275)
Both *haandi* and *karai* are round shaped vessels. As it is mentioned in the context, a *karai* is a huge round shaped vessel while a *haandi* is a small one.

(6) "Now will do fifty *baithuks*!" (180)
Baithuk is an Indian word. In the sentence it occurs with the plural suffix '-s'. It literally means, sitting down and then standing up in a continuous process. In the context it is employed as a means of punishment.

(7) "Keep walking through that *gully*, till you see the big advertisement for Amul Butter . . . " (175)
Gully is an Indian word which in Hindi refers to a narrow lane. From the context, it is evident that it is a pathway through which people can walk.

(8) "*Bhaji* and *chapati*. And my special *masala wada* with mango chutney . . . " (181)
Bhaji, *chapati*, *masala wada* and mango *chutney* are all Indian food items. In the supplement of Indian English, *Oxford Advanced Learners Dictionary*, 1999, the words *bhaji*, *chapati* and *wada* are enlisted. However, the food item *chutney* (pickles) is not listed. Other constructions, where the words occur in the novel are:
"Roopa rolled out fresh chapattis." (103)
"I'll make the chapatis, said Om. I'm the chapati champion." (397)
"Lets have *masala wada* today, proposed Ishvar." (399)

(9) "—and a package of jasmine *agarbatti*." (183)
Agarbatti in Hindi means incense sticks. The meaning of the word is not evident from the context. The religious concept and ritual of lighting of incense sticks is entirely Indian. The author touched on this concept in Indian English.

(10) "The *bhistee* will come when it's time for water."(346)

From the context it is not evident that *bhistee* is the man who carries water. However, it is apparent to the reader that the *bhistee* has something to do with water.

(11) "Maneck, will you stay and finish the box? Asked Mrs. Kohlah, as she was helped into the *palkhi*." (589)

The *palkhi* is a wooden enclosure with doors and suspended from two extended horizontal bars, which is carried on shoulders by four bearers. For the native English reader the meaning of the word is not stated in the context. However, it is clear that it is a means of transport on which people can travel.

(vi) Hybrid Indianism

Hybrid Indianism or mixed formations are Indianisms which consist of two or more elements, in which one element is from an Indian language and one from English. These are contextually restricted. The hybrid Indianisms found in Mistry's writings are unique. Moreover, the Indian words used in mixed formation have a wider usage in an Indian language than in Indian English.

(a) "She died on the same day of the *Shahenshahi calendar* as her husband." (26)
(b) "Omprakash broke the silence by pointing out a *watermelon-sherbet stand*." (7)
(c) "While Dukhi and the child slept, she crept out of the hut with a small *brass haandi* . . . ," (97)
(d) " . . . and replaced them with a *pukka house*." (136)
(e) "He saw their tired faces, how poor their clothes were, the *worn-out chappals*." (7)
(f) " . . . carried by disreputable *market place jyotshis*." (86)
(g) ". . . and a handful of injured *dockyard mathadis*." (259)
(h) "Like a *road side mavali*." (288)
(i) "Sounds like one more *government tamasha*." (5)
(j) "That's the goddess of protection. Her blessing is a business necessity. *Compulsory puja*." (309)

The novel *A Fine Balance* presents a range of social classes with varieties of Indian characters. The language of each of these classes from the beggar to the elite varies considerably. The language of the tailors is polite (evident from their vocative markers '*bai*' and '*ji*' as terms conveying respect) and mixed with a group of Indianisms. This group is associated with people who are uneducated, rural and live on hard-earned daily wages. Another group belongs to the urban uneducated poor of which Shankar is a member. The Shroff's and the Kohlah's belong to a separate class who are educated, urban and sophisticated in their life styles. Indianisms are found in each of these classes, the continuum is denser among the uneducated people and thinner among the educated, as in the following :

> Shankar: "o babu ek paisa day-ray." (7)
> Ishvar: "No, no, bas, we are full." (348)
> Om: "The government destroying our house for sure, . . . and working for Dinabai." (310)
> Mr. Kohlah: "You have no control over your son, . . . can you not do something about his non-stop keech-keech." (219)

4. Findings

Rohinton Mistry has made a conscious attempt to bring Indianisms in the speech of his characters. In specific situations the character's repertoire is better undersood and creates ambience for other members of the class if it contains Indianisms. The abundance of Indianisms in the speech of the uneducated classes probably imparts to it a whiff of authenticity. All the same, there is a lurking suspicion that it could be the author's way of saying that English for them is more of an alien linguistic space than for the educated classes.

It may be mentioned that mainstream English is characterised by its richness. Indian English has its peculiarities but it is not always main-stream. Authors from India seldom write on matters other than Indian, as in Vikram Seth's *An Equal Music* or Amitav Ghosh's *In an Antique Land*. They are main-stream now. Indian writers from outside the main-stream, writing just about India are usually looked at as anything else but Indian ethnic writers.

Gorlach Manfred in *Text Types and the History of English* states that English being a second language in India cannot be expected to exhibit the full range of styles, domains and text type (a specific linguistic pattern in which formal/structural characters have been conventionalised in a specific culture for certain well-defined and standard uses of language) (105). Thus, in such situations usually models and norms tend to be borrowed from outside (and sometimes garbed in Indian attire, in certain cases heavily, for example, in Mulk Raj Anand). After the analysis on *An Equal Music* and *A Fine Balance* it can be concluded that further studies can be done on a larger corpus, to show much variation within individual text types. The study tries to locate the linguistic features obligatory or expected in a specific text type and identify the mixed types.

Chapter - 6

Structural Features

1. Introduction

This chapter deals with the structural features of the verbs preceding complementisers and a syntactic discussion of complementisers from four novels of Amitav Ghosh. The chapter has two sections, namely semantics and syntax. Semantics is the study of relationships between words and meanings and syntax is the study of patterned relations of phrases and sentences. In the syntax section, the syntactic correlates of semantic features in Ghosh's fictional writings are considered. For the frequency of cognitive group of verbs in addition to two of Ghosh's novels four other were analysed. This is followed by findings from the analysis. The outline of this chapter is as follows :

1. Introduction
2. Semantics
3. Syntactic Correlates of Semantic Features
4. The Cognitive Group of Governing Verbs of the Complementiser "that"
5. Findings
6. Schematic Representation of the Cognitive Verbs Governing Complementisers
7. List of Verbs
8. List of Sentences with Complementisers

2. Semantics

Four novels of Amitav Ghosh published within a span of eighteen years are chosen for this analysis. These novels were explored for any remarkable, noticeable, conspicuous difference in the use of verbs as members of different verbal groups (Bandyopadhyay, "Complementisers"). For this purpose, a certain type of verb—verbs which govern complementisers in complement clauses was taken into consideration. "Complementiser" is a term introduced by Rosenbaum in 1967. While analysing subordinating and co-ordinating conjunctions he noticed that there was a big difference between "conjunction-that-like-subordinators" (e.g., that, whether, etc.) and subordinators like "although," "as," etc. He suggested the special term "complementiser" for the former. Though complementisers as a special set of subordinating conjunctions were first marked and separated from those outside the set by Rosenbaum, they have since undergone several modifications in the range, number and even designation of some of their elements (Van der Auwera, "Relative that"). This section deals with the following complementisers: that, if/whether, for and wh-.

De Boel in his study of complementisers in classical Attic writes that " . . . my (his) purpose is to show that complementisers, to a perhaps surprising extent, do carry distinctive meaning, and that this meaning is closely related to the concept of existential presupposition" ("Towards a Theory" 288). From his list of verbs that govern complements in Aristophanes' plays he found that "many of the governing verbs take more than one complementiser, and that in many cases, difference of complementiser choice brings about difference of meaning" (289).

In addition to the meaning and the question of more than one complementiser, this study explores the nature of the governing verbs in Indian writing in English. For this purpose Amitav Ghosh's four novels *The Circle of Reason*, *The Shadow Lines*, *The Calcutta Chromosome*, and *The Hungry Tide* (henceforth referred to as TCOR, TSL, TCC, and THT) are chosen and all the verbs governing the complementisers "that," "if/whether," "for" and "wh-" in these four novels are listed. From the list it appears that numerically the complementiser "that" is the largest in all the four novels (Table 6.1). Next, all the verbs are separated into lexico-semantic groups, e.g., the cognitive, the demonstrative, speech act, etc. (Table 6.2). The complementisers "if" and "for" being very few in number were not included in the analysis. The numbers for the complementisers "whether" and "wh-" do not tally as the same verb in different inflected forms occurs in the constructions. Table 6.3 gives verbs in the list that take more than one complementiser. Such verbs are seven in number: know, see, remember, say, tell, wonder, and decide.

Table 6.1

	that	*for*	*If/whether*	*Wh-*
TCOR	23	—	2	10
TCC	18	1	3	2
TSL	15	1	5	9
THT	7	5	3	4
Total	**63**	**7**	**13**	**25**

For convenience, the governing verbs are divided into monosemic and polysemic types and into those taking one or more complementisers. The complete list of verbs is shown in the verb list (In $ 6.8 are gathered together) the sentences from the four novels that were taken up for the analysis. The primary concern in this study being the group identification of the governing verbs, it is not taken into consideration whether the clause embedded by the complementiser is finite or non-finite; neither the force of the clause introduced by the complementisers: whether it is an interrogative or declarative or an irrealis clause (i.e., a clause denoting an 'unreal' or hypothetical event which has not yet happened and may never happen) (Radford, *English Syntax*) is reckoned on.

Table 6.2

		that	*If/whether*	*Wh-*
Cognitive	TCOR	11	2	4
	TCC	13	1	2
	TSL	12	2	7
	THT	5	3	4
Demonstrative	TCOR	—	—	1
Speech	TCOR	4	—	1
	TCC	4	—	—
	TSL	3	2	1
	THT	1	—	—
Others	TCOR	—	—	1
	TCC	1	—	—
	TSL	—	1	—
	THT	1	—	—

Table 6.3

	that	*Wh-*	*for*	*whether*
know	√	√	—	√
see	√	√	√	—
remember	√	√	—	—
say	√	—	—	√
tell	√	√	—	√
wonder	—	√	—	√
decide	√	—	—	—

The following cases are considered :

(i) Monosemic Verb with One Complementiser

(a) . . . even Gopal had to *admit that* there was a remarkable resemblance . . . (TCOR 22)

(b) 1. . . . he *noticed that* the word 'Lhasa' was prefixed by a symbol . . . (TCC 9)

2. . . . I *noticed that* she wasn't listening to me. (TSL 20)

(c) 1. He had *discovered that* rents . . . yield a better harvest. . . . (TCOR 60)

2. When I went in I *discovered that* my seat was directly behind the woodwind section. (TSL 14)

(d) 1. His teachers *decided* that he had a gift for history. (TCOR 40)
2. Tridib had once *decided that* he wanted to be an Air Raid Warden when he grew up. (TSL 51)

(e) It was lucky, he *said* afterwards *that* there is so much cloth to a dhoti. (TCOR 44)

In this case the single complementiser brings out the single meaning of the verb.

(ii) Monosemic Verb with Two or More Complementisers

(a) Tell

1. . . . Ava couldn't *tell that* she didn't exactly have his full attention. (TCC 4)
2. . . . it fell to Tridib to *tell* me . . . *how* Mrs Price's father . . . had left the farm . . . (TSL 51)
3. . . . he . . . wouldn't *tell* Tridib *how* he had come to learn them. (TSL 183)

Here two different complementisers governed by the same verb reveal a single meaning.

(iii) Polysemic Verb with One Complementiser

(a) Realize

1. After a few minutes he *realized that* her scrubbing was only making matters worse, . . . (TCC 147)
2. . . . my father had *realized that* the Shaheb had finally resolved the question . . . (TSL 41)
3. She had not *realized* then *that* on the Irrawady . . . she had also been protected . . . (THT 34)

With this verb the meaning of "understand" is displayed whereas the other meaning "convert into a fact" for instance *realize one's ambitions/hopes*, being inaccessible to complementiser structure, remains hidden.

(b) Recognize

. . . he *recognized* at once *that* they . . . were syphilitics. (TCC 126)

Here also one meaning "be aware" is revealed whereas the other "know (be able to), identify again (sb/sth) that one has seen, heard, etc., before," for example, *recognize a tune/an old acquaintance*, etc., cannot be accessed with a complementiser construction. This possibility (iii) was not considered as polysemic verbs with one complementiser cannot display more than one meaning.

(iv) Polysemic Verb with One Complementiser Displaying Two Meanings

(a) See

1. Gopal could *see that* Balaram was no less saddened than he was. (TCOR 51)
   (see = understand)
2. . . . Kanai *saw that* he had drawn out his daa. (THT 323)
   (see = be aware of by using the power of sight)

(b) Remember

1. . . . she tried *to remember how* it had looked. (TCOR 360)
   (remember = call back to the mind the memory of)
2. I *remember how* we listened to him . . . (TSL 197)
   (remember = to keep in mind for attention or consideration)

(c) Know

1. Just wanted *to know whether* there was . . . a staircase . . . here . . . (TSL 106)
   (know = discern)

2. . . . I don't *know whether* I will be able to do it. (TCOR 418)
(know = to be convinced or certain of)

(d) Wonder

1. Murugan hesitated, *wondering whether* he ought to make sure that Mrs. Aratourian was alright. (TCC 313)
(wonder = ask one self)
2. I used *to wonder* later *whether* this was merely a legacy of a child's foreshortened vision . . . (TSL 48)
(wonder = marvel, feel surprised)

For the polysemic verb "see" the same complementiser displays two meanings; it is to be noted that in (1) it is a verb of intellectual state, while in (2) it belongs to the group of perceptual verbs.

(v) Polysemic Verb with Two or More Complementisers Displaying One Meaning

(a) See

1. But he could *see that* she was afraid. (TCOR 32)
(see = understand)
2. . . . I don't *see how* it can be done. (TCOR 286)
(see = understand)
3. We'll just have to try to keep the whole thing quiet, and *see what* we can do.
(see = understand) (TCOR 258)

(vi) Polysemic Verb with Two or More Complementisers Displaying Two Meanings

(a) Know

1. Balaram *knew that* he had to say something. (TCOR 16)
(know = discern)

2. . . . I don't *know whether* I will be able to do it. (TCOR 418)
   (know = to be convinced or certain of)

(b) Wonder

1. They often *wondered what* happened to him . . .(TCC 13) (wonder = ask one self)
2. . . . she *wondered how* this young bird lover was taking the crowds . . . (TCC 313)
   (wonder = marvel; feel surprised)

(c) See

1. . . . I don't *see how* it can be done. (TCOR 286)
   (see = understand)
2. I had not expected *to see what* Tridib had seen. (TSL 57)
   (see = be aware of by using the power of sight)

(d) Remember

1. *Remember that* this is a place where the rates of malaria in the general population are. . . high . . . (remember= keep in the memory) (TCC 64)
2. I *remember how* we listened to him . . . (TSL 197)
   (remember = to keep in mind for attention or consideration)

From the above six categories the different semantic interpretations of monosemic and polysemic verbs occurring in the narration are brought into focus. It is interesting to note the applications of the same verbs with multiple interpretations in different contexts. (*Continued in $ 4*).

3. Syntactic Correlates of Semantic Features

From the study of the relation between the meaning of a predicate and its syntactic behaviour it is found that semantically related verbs govern the same sorts of complements and show similar properties. Predicates which are considered to be "semantically related" always share one essential semantic feature, a feature which is systematically associated with syntactic correlates.

This section discusses the semantic features which have syntactic correlates in the complementation system especially on the semantic classes of 'that' complementation system which conforms to the data collected from the novels of Amitav Ghosh.

The first relevant semantic class is that of emotive and/or evaluative predicates. These predicates express the subjective evaluation of a proposition by a subject, rather than knowledge of its truth-value. Examples of emotive and non-emotive predicates due to Kiparsky ("Fact") are :

(a) [+emotive] crazy, odd, sad, alarm, bother, a tragedy, regret, resent, deplore, urgent, vital, non-sense, unlikely, prefer.
(b) [-emotive] well-known, beware, be sure, make clear, forget, say, suppose, seem, probable, turnout, believe, etc.

Among the syntactic properties of emotive verbs, is their ability to take a "for-to" infinitive complement and to allow the use of the subjunctive mood in their that-complement clause (". . . it was difficult *for* me *to* forgive my own stupidity. . ." TSL 218).

A second relevant semantic dimension in the complementation system is factivity (*cf.* Kiparsky). Factive predicates are those that presuppose the truth of their complements. The complement of a factive verb is, ontologically speaking, a fact, rather than merely a proposition.

A non-exhaustive list of factive (f) predicates is :

(i) f-verbs: regret, resent, forget, amuse, suffice, bother, care, admit, comment, emphasise, inform, know, mention, point out, recognise

(ii) realise, find out, discover, know, learn, observe, perceive, recall, remember, reveal, see
(iii) f-adjectives: significant, odd, strange, interesting

Karttunen ("Some Observations") claims that true factives, like those in (a) express some emotion or subjective attitude about the complement proposition. This is why most true factives are also emotive/evaluative.

F-verbs differ in interesting ways in propositional (p) verbs. As their name implies, these verbs are characterised by the fact that ontological type of their complement is a proposition. The class of propositional verbs includes speech act verbs (i.e., verbs of linguistic communication) assert, say, tell, etc., and verbs of propositional attitude—traditionally called verbs of intellectual state, Quirk *et al.* (*A Grammar*), believe, think, etc., examples are listed below :

1. p-verbs: allege, assert, assume, believe, claim, conclude, conjecture, consider, decide, declare, envisage, estimate, fancy, feel, figure, imagine, intimate, judge, propose, report, reckon, say, state, suggest, suppose, suspect, tell, think
2. p-adjectives: likely, possible

There are several syntactic properties which are sensitive to the factive/propositional difference. First, f-complements generally require the 'that' complementiser, although this requirement is not so strong in some cases. In contrast p-verbs may appear with a null complementiser. The list of verbs governing the complementiser 'that' in the three novels (TCOR, TCC and TSL) have been divided into f-, p-, +e and –e verbs and are as follows :

TCOR

f	know, notice, see, remember, realize, discover
p	tell, decide, think, say, hear

TCC	
f	know, notice, discover, see, remember, realize
p	tell, imagine, believe, assume, assert
-e	believe

TSL	
f	discover, see, notice, realize, know
p	tell, believe, decide, claim, assume
-e	forget, believe

From the above data, it is evident that the f- and p- verbs in the three novels TCOR, TCC and TSL are more or less identical and also equal in number (ignoring the multiple occurrence of the same verb). However, no tangible conclusion can be drawn about the use of these verbs in these three works of fiction.

4. The Cognitive Group of Governing Verbs of the Complementiser "that"

From Table 6.2 and also from section 7 showing the list of verbs governing the complementisers in the four novels it is found that the cognitive group is the dominant one. An exhaustive list of such verbs, consisting primarily of the 'private' type of factual verbs expressing intellectual states such as 'belief' and intellectual acts such as 'discovery' is given in Quirk *et al.* (*A Comprehensive Grammar* 1181).

These verbs were further analysed for frequency of occurrence in the following four Indian English novels and for the sake of comparison in two novels by native British authors:

1. *The Circle of Reason* by Amitav Ghosh
2. *The Shadow Lines* by Amitav Ghosh
3. *English, August* by Upamanyu Chatterjee
4. *The God of Small Things* by Arundhati Roy
5. *Arthur and George* by Julian Barnes
6. *Yellow Dog* by Martin Amis

The results of the analysis are given in Table 6.4 : the frequency of occurrence decreasing downwards.

Table 6.4

TSL	*TCOR*	*EA*	*AG*	*TGOST*	*YD*
Know	Know	Know	Know	Know	Know
Believe	Decide	Realise	Think	Realise	Think
Discover	Discover	Feel	Realise	Believe	Believe
Think	Think	Believe	Believe	Think	Remember
Understand	Remember	Think	Decide	Notice	Realise
Decide	Understand	Decide	Imagine	Decide	Understand
Remember		Remember	Discover	Sense	
Notice		Sense	Understand	Imagine	

This corpus-based functional analysis shows that

1. the verb *know* has the highest frequency of all;
2. other high frequency verbs are *think, believe*;
3. some verbs have a low frequency;
4. some verbs occur only once or twice in a novel;
5. of the top frequency verbs, about a dozen in number

   (a) *know* and *think* occur in all the six novels;
   (b) *believe* and *decide* in five;
   (c) *realise, understand* and *remember* in four; and
   (d) *discover, notice, sense, imagine* and *find* in two.

From Table 6.4 it is obvious that for romantic fiction of about 300-400 pages the most used cognitive governing verbs of the complementiser 'that' by both Indian English and native British authors are about a dozen in number and remarkably similar. The data from Table 6.4 though based on only six novels appear significant enough to merit consideration. The Table demonstrates that a certain linguistic feature of Indian English creative writing, being similar or identical in part to that of native British creative writing, cannot but testify to the fact that it is a variant of International Standard English.

It may now be possible to venture the following hypothesis :

> "In a romantic fiction of 300-400 pages written in a native or non-native variety of English the number of most used (high frequency) cognitive governing verbs of the complemestiser 'that' is about a dozen."

5. Findings

Amitav Ghosh's four novels *TCOR, TSL, TCC and THT* offered a fair number (about 120) of complementisers ("that," "if/ whether," "for," "wh-") for the study. Of these "if" and "for" were very few in number and so were not taken up for consideration. It was found that :

1. Complementiser "that" was the dominant one, that is, much larger in number (45) than the others.
2. Monosemic governing verbs take one or more than one complementiser (say . . . that/whether, tell . . . that/ whether) indicating that difference of complementiser choice does not always bring about difference of meaning. This is also true for some polysemic verbs (see . . . that/how/what = understand; remember . . . how/when = call back to the mind the memory of, recollect; know . . . whether/what = to be convinced or certain of).
3. For some polysemic verbs, a change in complementiser choice displays, unlike (2) above, a change in meaning. Thus: see . . . that (= understand) and see . . . whether (= be aware of by the power of sight); remember . . . that (keep in memory) and remember . . . how/when (= call back to the mind the memory of, recollect); know . . . what/whether (= to be convinced or certain of) and know . . . that (= discern, perceive directly).
4. The polysemic "see" with the same complementiser reveals a change in meaning : "be aware of by using the power of sight" and "understand" : here the verb changes

its group from a verb of perception to one of intellectual state.

5. Of all the governing verbs the cognitive group (including the sub-groups of verbs of intellectual state : believe, find, imagine, reckon, think; perceptual verbs : see, notice; verbs of encounter : discover, find; retrospective verbs: remember, remind; verbs of negative meaning : doubt; etc.) is the largest.
6. Through an analysis of the frequency of occurrence of the most used cognitive governing verbs of the complementiser 'that' in four Indian English and two native British novels it was found that this linguistic feature conforms to the syntactic conventions of international Standard English.

6. Schematic Representation of the Cognitive Verbs Governing Complementisers

Finally, from dictionary definitions of the verbs given below, the network of cognitive verbs governing complementisers in the four novels can be schematically represented as :

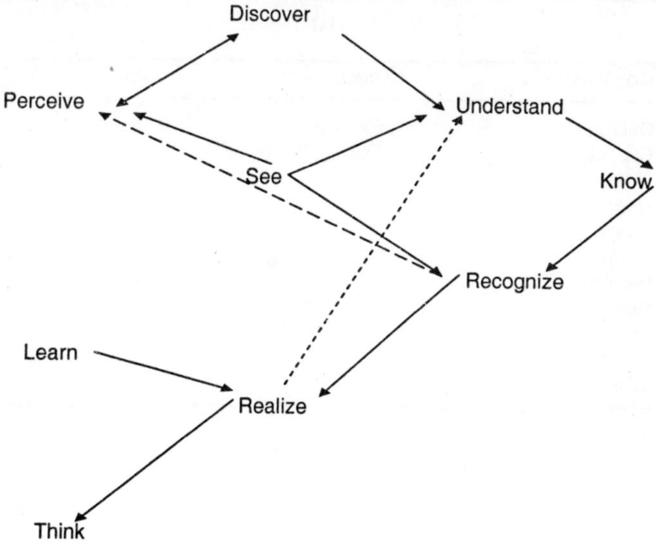

See = understand, perceive/(eye), discover, recognize
Discover = perceive/(eye), understand, recognize
Know = perceive directly, recognize, have in the mind, realize
Recognize = perceive, realize
Realize = understand, think

7. List of Verbs

Groups of verbs culled from the four novels TCOR, TCC, TSL and THT.

TCOR

Cognitive	*Speech*	*Demonstrative*
1. Believe	1. Acknowledge	1. Describe
2. Decide	2. Admit	
3. Discover	3. Explain	
4. Doubt	4. Say	
5. Hear	5. Tell	
6. Know		
7. Notice		
8. Realise		
9. Reckon		
10. Remember		
11. See		
12. Think		
13. Wonder		

THT

Cognitive	*Speech*	*Others*
1. Decide	1. Explain	1. See
2. Expect	2. Tell	
3. Guess		
4. Hear		
5. Imagine		
6. Know		
7. Realise		
8. See		
9. Think		
10. Understand		
11. Wonder		

TCC

	Cognitive	Speech	Others
1.	Assume	1. Admit	1. See
2.	Believe	2. Assert	
3.	Discover	3. Swear	
4.	Expect	4. Tell	
5.	Find		
6.	Guess		
7.	Imagine		
8.	Know		
9.	Notice		
10.	Realise		
11.	Recall		
12.	Recognise		
13.	Remember		
14.	Think		
15.	Wonder		

TSL

	Cognitive	Speech
1.	Accept	
2.	Assume	1. Ask
3.	Believe	2. Claim
4.	Decide	3. Explain
5.	Discover	4. Tell
6.	Forget	
7.	Gather	
8.	Hear	
9.	Imagine	
10.	Know	
11.	Notice	
12.	Realize	
13.	Recall	
14.	Remember	
15.	See	
16.	Understand	
17.	Wonder	

8. List of Sentences with Complementisers

TCOR

That-complementiser

1. . . . it was generally reckoned that the boy's arrival was the real beginning. (3)

2. Balaram knew that he had to say something. (16)
3. . . . even Gopal had to admit that there was a remarkable resemblance . . . (22)
4. Balaram did not leave his study or even acknowledge that he had heard her. (24)
5. When the lights were switched on, a few people noticed that Ma Saraswati . . . looked a little pained. (30)
6. But he could see that she was afraid. (32)
7. He had been told that every year they flew across the continent to winter in that lake. (37)
8. . . . he knew, too, that acquiescence could buy safety for his own . . . (38)
9. His teachers decided that he had a gift for history. (40)
10. Gopal could see that Balaram was no less saddened than he was. (51)
11. . . . . he said, some people think it rational to believe that events don't have a meaning. (87)
12. Some of his regular customers turned him away saying that there had been a shift in the political climate. (109)
13. It will help us to remember that we cannot limit the benefits of our education and learning to ourselves. (117)
14. You can show them to Bhudeb-babu and tell him that he doesn't have to come. (135)
15. Do you know that he's kidnapped my wife . . . (139)
16. . . . Joyti saw that they were in a large, high-ceilinged room . . . (166)
17. You had only to look at him to know that the whole thing was beyond him now. (315)
18. . . . he realized at last that he was lost. (316)
19. Do you remember that one time when you came to me at night . . . (318)
20. . . . she had heard somewhere that a sambuq called Zeynab was to sail for the Red Sea . . . (333)
21. Later he discovered that at that moment Virat Singh had asked Zindi . . . (366)

22. . . . it . . . staggered him to think that this very country had survived one of the most savage wars of this century. (376)
23. Gopal was busy with a client . . . when his peer interrupted to tell him that Balaram had arrived. (51)

Wh- complementisers

1. They often wondered what had happened to him. . .(13)
2. I know what you are, said Balaram . . . (69)
3. . . . its only Sri Krishna reminding you what the world's like. (122)
4. . . . she'll beat you up once she knows what you did. (187)
5. And now I know what the answer is . . . (219)
6. We'll just have to try to keep the whole thing quiet, and see what we can do. (285)
7. . . . I don't see how it can be done. (286)
8. . . . she wondered how this young bird lover was taking the crowds . . . (313)
9. He described . . .what he had said . . . (314)
10. . . . she tried to remember how it had looked. (360)

Whether

1. . . . a microbiologist . . . checks it to see whether anything's gone wrong . . . (412)
2. . . . I don't know whether I'll be able to do it. (418)

TCC

That-complementiser

1. . . . Ava couldn't tell that she didn't exactly have his full attention. (4)
2. He could have sworn that she was actually startled. . . (6)
3. . . . he noticed that the word 'Lhasa' was prefixed by a symbol . . . (9)
4. He looked over his shoulder and discovered that the pale outline of an enormous white triangle had begun to materialize . . . (9)

5. He was relieved to see that she wasn't home yet . . . (11)
6. At first he had expected that the building would fill up around him . . . (13)
7. Mistaken are those who imagine that silence is without life . . . (24)
8. . . . she thought it endearing that someone . . . should take such evident pleasure in talking to people . . . (24)
9. . . . Murugan had been known to admit that his interest in this rather obscure subject had initially had a biographical origin. (30)
10. Murugan believed that the development in malaria research . . . and the break through in . . . were the most important advances in the subject . . . (31-32)
11. She remembered hearing that Romen Halder had started with nothing . . . (56)
12. Remember that this is a place where the rates of malaria in the general population are . . . high . . . (54)
13. But she's very sharp you know and I often find that it helps to talk things over with her. (93)
14. . . . he recognized at once that they . . . were syphilitics. (126)
15. After a few minutes she realized that her scrubbing was only making matters worse . . . (147)
16. . . . her friends assumed that this was merely a manner of speaking . . . (177)
17. . . . she asserted that it was Mme. Salminen who had revealed to her the truth . . . (177)
18. . . . he guessed that the station-master had reached the point . . . (226)

Wh-complmentisers

1. I know what they're doing . . . (5)
2. He scratched his head trying to recall what he had done with the machine. (98)

Whether

1. Murugan hesitated, wondering whether he ought to make sure that Mrs. Aratounian was alright. (133)

2. . . . she had a moment of panic, wondering whether there was a fire somewhere within. (135)
3. Antar watched worriedly wondering whether he'd do any damage. (185)

For-complementiser

1. But for that to work they have to create a single perfect moment of discovery . . . (253)

TSL

That-complementiser

1. . . . he told them that he had been to stay with old Mrs. Price, . . . (11)
2. When she'd heard that Tridib's father was ill she had written to them . . . (13)
3. When I went in I discovered that my seat was directly behind the woodwind section. (14)
4. . . . I could see that those names, . . . were to me a set of magical talismans . . . (20)
5. . . . I noticed that she wasn't listening to me. (20)
6. . . . she would not have believed that there really were people like Tridib . . . (30)
7. . . . my father had realized that the Shaheb had finally resolved the question . . . (41)
8. . . . we knew that they had gone outside, back to the terrace. (47)
9. Tridib had once decided that he wanted to be an Air Raid Warden when he grew up. (51)
10. He . . . always claimed that he injured himself in a motorcycle accident. (63)
11. . . . we're willing to accept that you're . . . horrified by the badness of the big city. (84)
12. I gathered that he had become something of a minor celebrity among them, . . . (98)
13. My mother . . . explained . . . that my grandmother had started a course of Ayurvedic treatment . . . (118)
14. . . . we ought not to forget that he had been quick to turn the other way . . . (129)

15. . . . we'll have to assume that you imagined the whole thing. (222)

Wh-complementisers

1. I tried to recall for her how, when we were eight-year-old children, she . . . had invented London for me. (32)
2. . . . he knew what he wanted to do . . . (52)
3. . . . I wonder what you'll have to say to him . . . (53)
4. . . . he could not imagine what it would be like . . . (67)
5. I remember how I shouted at her . . . (78)
6. I can't understand why you're defending her. (79)
7. I waited, not daring to believe what she had said. (80)
8. He . . . wouldn't tell Tridib how he had come to learn them. (183)
9. . . . we recall . . . how we'd stood at street-corners, taking collections and selling little paper flags. (220)

Whether

1. I don't know whether you care for that kind of thing? (16)
2. . . . I asked . . . whether the snake was of the species Boidae . . . (28)
3. I listened to him bewildered, wondering whether I would ever know anything at all . . . (30)
4. Could you tell me . . . whether this is where the Left Book Club used to be . . . (30)
5. . . . I'd wanted to see whether they were real. (71)

For-complementiser

1. . . . it was difficult for me to forgive my own stupidity. (218)

THT

That-complementiser

1. . . . it would be strange . . . to think that this was the threshold of the Sundarbans . . . (9)
2. She realized that on the Irrawaddy . . . she had also been protected . . . (34)

3. . . . she guessed that this was where the . . . dinner was . . . cooked. (83)
4. She explained that in recent weeks the government had been stepping up the pressure on the settlers . . . (223)
5. . . . he had expected that the sight of it would trigger, . . . (270)
6. He does not understand that when a party comes to power, it must govern . . . (275)
7. . . . Kanai saw that he had drawn out his daa. (325)

Wh-complementisers

1. the . . . masters were keenly awaiting . . . to see what the future might hold. (144)
2. . . . it occurred to him to wonder why in English, silence is commonly said to 'fall' or 'descend' . . . (154)
3. When he heard why I was there, he said he would help . . . (163)
4. Can you imagine what he'd do if he was taken on to a plane? (268)

Whether

1. Briefly he wondered whether he ought to tell her that there was a special compartment for women. (5)
2. . . . the authorities were keen to know whether he had picked up anything of interest . . . (77)
3. . . . it was up to him to decide whether he would back down . . . (323)

For-complementiser

1. . . . it was out of character for her to ask favour. (19)
2. It took a while for Kanai and Nilima to make their way . . . (59)
3. It would serve no purpose for her to meet with Nilima. (201)
4. It would be good for him to hear it from you . . . (257)
5. I don't know if it'll be . . . possible for you to stay here. (398)

Chapter - 7

Conclusion

Even though English is a non-native language, it is adopted in India as the language of education and literary expression and as an important medium of communication amongst the people of various regions. Mulk Raj Anand, R. K. Narayan and Raja Rao who began to write in the early thirties of the last century were among the earliest Indian novelists writing in English. But it was only in the 1980s and 1990s that there appeared a group of talented writers who produced major literary works in Indian English admired not only in the English speaking world but also beyond it as corroborated by ensuing translations which followed. Salman Rushdie's *Midnight's Children* won the Booker Prize in 1981 while Vikram Seth's *The Golden Gate* published in 1986 won worldwide acclaim. The post-Rushdiean era dawned with a new awakening of Indian writing in English with a distinct voice and expression. During this period, Indian writers started using English without any sense of nostalgia and so to say as a foreign tool very much tempered and honed in their own workshops. A "chutneyfication" (to use a Rushdiean term) took place in the process of Indianisation of English where the tight language structure yielded to flexibility and synchronised itself with the local colour and flavour. The work has attempted to study the Indianisation of English by an analysis of some significant linguistic features in selected post-1980 Indian English fiction.

1. Brief Summary of the Chapters

Chapter 1, "Introduction," discussed Indian English, its various registers, origin, definition and characteristics. Indian English was defined as the term for the form of English used in India. By Indians, it is learned and used as a second language. There are more than thirty million speakers of English in India. The domains of its use noted in the study are government administration, law, the military, higher education, commerce, and the media. With the status of a second language, it serves the international role of medium of communication with the global community of nations and intra-national and intra-regional roles of link language among diverse linguistic habitats. In the bilingual speech community the function for the use of English is formal rather than informal or intimate. The section on "Educated Indian English" tried to elaborate this point. Similarly, the section on "Some Aspects of Style and Language in Earlier Indian English Fiction" illustrated the features of Indianisation in the novels of Mulk Raj Anand, Raja Rao and R. K. Narayan. From the review, the first creative work in Indian English fiction was found to be Bankim Chandra Chatterjee's *Rajmohon's Wife* which appeared as a serial in the weekly *Indian Field* in 1864 and was published as a book only in 1935. The origins of Indian English were traced from Southern and Northern British English and American English. "The Origins of Indian English" discussed these points from Zacharias Thundy's study. "English in India" mentioned two aspects of Indian English that brought the speech form from the state of pidgin to the state of second language.

In Chapter 2, entitled "Review of Literature," a survey of previously published literature on Indian English was made. Earlier articles and publications brought in focus were from the late fifties till the year two thousand and five. In this chapter, the works done by S. V. Parasher, Braj B. Kachru, Larry E. Smith, Kamal K. Sridhar, S. N. Sridhar, Yamuna Kachru, Rodney F. Moag, C. J. Daswani, Bh. Krishnamurthy, Ramesh Mohan, Sivendra K. Verma, Rani Rubdy, and R. Burchfield were discussed. It was noted that analysts and scholars have previously stressed on the lexicon, phonology, word formation, and syntactic features of Indian English corpus found from the domains of education, government administration, and media. There exists a number of publications on these fields from the late seventies. These were mentioned in detail in the chapter. It was found that Parasher's *Indian English Functions and Form* described the variety of English which had co-existed with several Indian languages and was thus 'X-ized' or nativised and which in course of time became a non-native variety of English. Indian variety of English showed certain differences. These deviations were in determiners, modifiers, verb patterns, auxiliaries, prepositions, etc. In this context, it was found that for Braj B. Kachru, the linguistic study of the features of the deviant variety in a typically Indian context were register variation, style variation, collocation deviation, semantic shifts and lexical change. Kamal K. Sridhar and S. N. Sridhar have argued in terms of second language acquisition theory and discussed the target of acquisition, the input of the acquisition process, the role of the acquired language motivation of the learners and lexical and pragmatic aspects of second language acquisition. Other scholars had studied the aspects of style and language in Indian English fiction in the past. The review noted Rani Rubdy's classification of the language under the areas of syntax, lexico-semantics, and cohesion. The chapter ended with the findings on the earlier works on Indian English. The focus of this study has been directed on different characteristic features of Indian English based on phonology, lexicon, semantics, and syntax, from the data available from the contemporary Indian English fiction. Phonological features were discussed in the next chapter.

Chapter 3, "Phonological Features," began with a brief review of the previous works on Indian English phonology. The variations in vowel utterances were scrutinised from Indian English fiction and discussed according to the General English pronunciation. The section on "Indian English Pronunciation" focused on the phonetic features of Indian English. The intonation patterns of selected sentences from Rohinton Mistry's novel *Such a Long Journey* were analysed in the section

"Intonation and Indian English." The dimensions of meaning associated with contour variation, found from the study, were mapped against six factors of emotional meaning. Attitudinal function, discourse function and grammatical function were discussed in "Functions of Intonation" section. From the study, "Variations in Vowel Utterances in Indian English," it was found that there were qualitative differences in five vowels (as represented in the fiction, *Such a Long Journey*). Other Indian English phonetic features were fast speech-tempo with choppy syllables, rhythmic variation in speech and stress. The variations in pronunciation were due to L1 influence, educational background and contact with English. Indians looked at their rich phonology for the nearest approximation of English phonemes and followed English pronunciation as it appeared through the English spelling. Most foreigners considered Indians to be much better speakers of good English than most other people including the Chinese, the Japanese, the Italian or the French. A study of the intonation pattern revealed that the constituents of the tone unit (the basic unit of intonation) were mostly the nucleus, the head, the pre-head and the tail. However, many sentences did not have pre-heads in their utterances. The variables of the contours of intonation taken for the study were range (wide/narrow), pitch reached at the end of the contour (high/mid/low) and shape of contour (one direction/with a change of direction). The next discussion was on Lexical Features.

Chapter 4, "Lexical Features," was about words and expressions of Indian origin in contemporary Indian English fiction. The authors whose writings were selected for this study were Arundhati Roy, Upamanyu Chatterjee, Vikram Chandra, Manju Kapur, Salman Rushdie, Amitav Ghosh, Vikram Seth and Rohinton Mistry. The chapter discussed kinds of borrowing, classification of borrowed words and semantic changes in word formation. It listed one hundred forty four borrowed words from Seth's *A Suitable Boy* with linguistic and semantic interpretations. Words of Indian origin from *Midnight's Children* were listed in the following section. The kinds of borrowing discussed were loan words, borrowing, loan translation and loan creation. The number of words borrowed from Indian languages into English in the last two decades is larger than what was found to be borrowed in the 1960s and 1970s. The words borrowed have fitted well in the English language. Most of them from Hindi and Urdu were without their original gender distinction markers. The words were nouns, adjectives and verbs. In semantic changes in word formation, the categories discussed were generalisation, specialisation, transference, degeneration, and the interjection 'arrey.' Five different authors in six Indian English novels had used the interjection with different spellings. Its distinctive semantic interpretations were intimacy/affection, non-agreement/anger, frustration, discovery/surprise, declaration/assertion, expostulation, cordiality in interrogation, and objection/censure. In the novel *A Suitable Boy*, the non-English nouns occurred with the English definite and indefinite articles. The verbs borrowed from Hindi, Urdu and Bengali were found in inflected and uninflected forms. The adjectives were uninflected according to number and gender. Compound nouns were a major category of borrowed words in *Midnight's Children*. It is finally noted that there were some common borrowed words in both the novels. Three functional features (characteteristic of Indian English) were discussed in the next chapter.

Chapter 5, "Functional Features," focused on these features in Indian English fiction. The chapter dealt with the phenomenon of repetition in conversational extracts from Vikram Seth's two novels, *A Suitable Boy* and *An Equal Music*, the feature cliché from Indian English fiction and the aspect of Indianism from Mistry's *A Fine Balance*. Eight categories of the use of repetition were found from the fiction which were : (1) as a rejoinder to provocation, (2) to avoid a direct answer, (3) to express disbelief or surprise, (4) to express appreciation, (5) tc stall and to gain time to formulate a proper answer, (6) to get or to keep the floor, (7) to request clarification, and (8) to request confirmation.

The aspects of repetition discussed in the chapter were associated with some sets of verbs of the same lexico-semantic group. The groups found were (i) annoy, irritate, tease, (ii) relish, appreciate, enjoy, savour, and (iii) distrust, disbelieve, doubt. There were more repetitions in *An Equal Music* than in the fiction *A Suitable Boy*. Self-repetition and allo-repetition were almost equal in number (eight and ten respectively). Among the eight categories, self-repetition and allo-repetition both occurred in (1) as a rejoinder to provocation and in (3) to express disbelief and surprise. The repetitions from *A Suitable Boy* were allo-repetitions. The findings were presented in Table 5.1.

In the section on cliché, the six types discussed were simile, multi-word expressions: literal translations from Indian languages, verb, adjective+ noun combinations, circumlocution, and vogue expressions.

In "Indianisms," the topics of discussion were transfer of context, transfer of L1 meanings to L2, transfer of form context component, grammatical deviations, Indian expressions and terms, and hybrid Indianism. The next feature of Indian English in the discussion was structural features.

Chapter 6, "Structural Features," was based on four of the novels of Amitav Ghosh, namely, *The Circle of Reason*, *The Shadow Lines*, *The Calcutta Chromosome* and *The Hungry Tide*. In the first section, semantics, the linguistic feature 'complementiser' was categorised into five sections according to different semantic interpretation of monosemic and polysemic verbs in complement clauses. In this analysis of complementisers in Amitav Ghosh's four novels, monosemic governing verbs were found to take more than one complementiser proving that not all complementisers carry distinctive meaning. The complementisers 'that', 'if /whether', 'for' and 'wh-' were taken for analysis. It was found that 'that' dominated all other complementisers in all the four novels. The complementisers 'if' and 'for' being very few in number were not considered in the analysis. Four lexico-semantic groups of verbs governing complementisers were found. The cognitive group was the largest, demonstrative and speech act verbs were the other notable groups. The findings were mentioned under six points in the conclusion. Some, verbs in the novels occurred with more than one complementiser. Such verbs were seven in number. They were: know, see, remember, say, tell, wonder and decide. The complete list of the verbs was shown in the 'Verb list' (§ 6.7).

The section on "Syntactic Correlates of Semantic Features" lists the verbs governing the complementiser "that" from four novels of Amitav Ghosh according to factive, propositional, +e (emotive) and –e verbs. It was found that in three novels, namely, TCOR, TCC and TSL the author had used almost the same group of factive and propositional verbs. List of sentences with complementisers represented the sentences from the four novels that were taken up for the analysis *Cf.* (§ 6.8).

In section 6.4, the frequency of the most used cognitive governing verbs of the complementiser 'that' was studied in detail. The results were shown in Table 6.4.

There was a schematic representation of the network of verbs governing complementisers in the four novels (§ 6.5). The complementiser distribution was illustrated by three Tables, 6.1, 6.2 and 6.3.

2. Limitations of the Work

This book could not accommodate certain works of fiction by some notable writers like Naipaul, Jhumpa Lahiri, Kiran Desai for some obvious reasons. V. S. Naipaul, for instance, a third generation Indian from the West Indies was not classified under Indian Writing in English though, he evokes ideas of homeland, rootlessness and his own personal feelings towards India in many of his books. Similarly, Jhumpa Lahiri, a Pulizer Prize winner from the United States was a writer uncomfortable with the label of Indian Writing in English.

Other contemporary Indian authors in English who were not included in the analysis are Anita Desai, Manohar Malgonkar,

Kamala Markandaya, Nayantara Sahgal, Kasthuri Sreenivasan, A. K. Ramanujan, Shobha De, Shashi Deshpande and Kamala Das. The reasons for not including the authors mentioned above are varied. Mostly these writers did not fit the following parameters chosen for the framework of this study.

Firstly, the study concentrated on the period nineteen eighties till two thousand five. The analysis was done from the data collected from fictional writings of the authors who began their careers during the last two decades and gained recognition.

Secondly, all the authors chosen were with Indian backgrounds. And thus the novels that dealt with India wholly or partly were taken up for the work as the topic of research is on "Indianisation of English."

Thirdly, the authors chosen were taken as representatives from each of the four regions of India, namely, the north, the west, the south and the east. Accordingly, Vikram Seth and Salman Rushdie represent the north, Rohinton Mistry, the west, Amitav Ghosh and Upamanyu Chatterjee, the east, and Arundhati Roy, the south.

Fourthly, the writings chosen are strongly based on Indian culture and society and the characters are Indian (even though non-native characters are also present). The data was found to ideally suit for the range on which the chapters are based. The selection of the authors was restricted to some extent for the purpose.

Finally, the parameters were not drawbacks for the overall study. Rather they are the pointers through which the research could be efficiently carried out on the available research materials in the prescribed time frame.

Bibliography

Alam, Q. Z. "The Cliché and Indian English Fiction." *Indianisation of English Language and Literature*. Ed. R. S. Pathak. New Delhi: Bahri Publications, 1994. 50-58.

Amis, Martin. *Yellow Dog*. London: Vintage, 2004.

Anand, Mulk Raj. *Coolie*. Delhi: Orient Paperbacks, 1972.

——. "Some Notes on Indian English Writing." *Studies in Australian and Indian Literature*. Eds. C. D. Narasimhaiah and S. Nagarajan. New Delhi: ICCR, 1971. 228-48.

Bandyopadhyay, Sumana. "Complementizers in Amitav Ghosh's *The Circle of Reason* and *The Calcutta Chromosome*." The 28th All India Conference of Linguistics. Banaras Hindu University, Varanasi. 2 November, 2006.

——."Indianisms in Rohinton Mistry's *A Fine Balance*." *Language Forum* 34.2 (2008) : 35-47.

——. "Present Continuous in Anurag Mathur's *The Inscrutable Americans*." (Under publication).

——. "Repetitions in the Conversational Extracts in Vikram Seth's *An Equal Music*." *Praci-Bhasha-Vijnan Indian Journal of Linguistics* 24 (2005): 77-89.

Bansal, R. K. *Intelligibility of Indian English*. Hyderabad: CIEFL, 1969.

——."Spoken English in India." *Bulletin of the Central Institute of English* 6 (1966-67): 6-97.

——."The Pronunciation of English in India." *Studies in the Pronunciation of English: A Commemorative Volume in Honour of A.C. Gimson*. Ed. S. Ramsaran. London: Routledge, 1990. 219-30.

Bansal, R. K., and J. Harrison. *Spoken English for India. A Manual of Speech and Phonetics*. Madras: Orient Longman, 1983.

Barnes, Julian. *Arthur and George*. London: Vintage, 2007.

Bayer, Josef. "Final Complementizers in Hybrid Languages." *Journal of Linguistics* 35 (1999): 233-71.

Bharucha, Nilufer E. "Articulating Silences? Rohinton Mistry's *A Fine Balance*." *Critical Practice* 5.1 (1998): 21-32.

Bokamba, E. G. "The Africanization of English." *The Other Tongue*. Ed. Braj. B. Kachru. Urbana, IL: University of Illinois Press, 1982. 77-98.

Bolinger, Dwight. "Intonation and its Use." *Melody in Grammar and Discourse*. Stanford: Stanford University Press, 1989.

——.ed. *Intonation: Selected Readings*. England: Penguin Books, 1972.

Burchfield, R., ed. *The Cambridge History of the English Language: English in Britain and Overseas; Origins and Development*. Vol. 5. Cambridge: Cambridge University Press, 1994.

Celce-Murcia, M., Z. Dornyei, and S. Thurrell. "Communicative Competence: A Pedagogically Motivated Model with Content Specification." *Issues in Applied Linguistics* 6. 2 (1995): 5-35.

Chandra, Vikram. *Love and Longing in Bombay*. Boston: Little Brown & Company, 1997.

——. *Red Earth and Pouring Rain*. New Delhi: Penguin Books, 1995.

Chatterjee, Bankim Chandra. *Rajmohan's Wife: Bankim Rachanavali*. Vol. 3. Calcutta: Sahitya Samsad, 1998. 1-88.

Chatterjee, Upamanyu. *English, August: An Indian Story*. New Delhi: Penguin Books, 2002.

——. *The Last Burden*. London: Faber and Faber, 1993.

Chaudhary, S. C. *Some Aspects of the Phonology of Indian English*. Ranchi : Jayaswal Press, 1989.

Chomsky, Noam, and Morris Halle. *The Sound Pattern of English*. New York : Harper and Row, 1968.

Clark, T. W., ed. *The Novel in India: Its Birth and Development*. Berkeley and Los Angeles: University of California, 1970.

Couper-Kuhlen, Elizabeth. *An Introduction to English Prosody*. Maryland : Edward Arnold, 1986.

Cruttenden, Alan. *Intonation*. Cambridge: Cambridge University Press, 1986.

Crystal, David. "The Intonation System of English." *Intonation: Selected Readings*. Ed. Dwight Bolinger. England: Penguin, 1972. 110-36.

Daswani, C. J. "Some Theoretical Implications for Investigating Indian English." *Indian Writing in English*. Ed. Ramesh Mohan. Madras: Orient Longman, 1978. 116-28.

De Boel, Gunnar. "Towards a Theory of the Meaning of Complementizers in Classical Attic." *Lingua* 52 (1980): 285-304.

Dumitrescu, D. "Rhetorical *vs.* Nonrhetorical Allo-Repetition: The Case of Romanian Interrogatives." *Journal of Pragmatics* 26 (1996): 321-54.

Dustoor, P. E. *The World of Words*. Bombay: Asia Publishing House, 1968.

Fanon, Frantz. *The Wretched of the Earth*. London: Penguin Books, 1990.

Ferrara, K. "Repetition as Rejoinder in Therapeutic Discourse: Echoing and Mirroring." *Repetition in Discourse: Interdisciplinary Perspectives*. Ed. B. Johnstone. Vol. 2. New Jersey: Ablex Publishing Corporation, 1994. 66-83.

Ghosh, Amitav. *In an Antique Land*. New Delhi: Ravi Dayal Publisher, 2001.

——. *The Calcutta Chromosome*. New Delhi: Ravi Dayal Publisher, 2005.

——. *The Circle of Reason*. New Delhi: Ravi Dayal Publisher, 2003.

——. *The Hungry Tide*. New Delhi: Harper Collins Publishers, 2005.

——. *The Shadow Lines*. New Delhi: Ravi Dayal Publisher, 2003.

Gimson, A. C. *An Introduction to the Pronunciation of English*. London: The English Language Book Society and Edward Arnold Ltd., 1970.

Goffin, R. C. *Some Notes on Indian English*. Oxford: Clarendon Press, 1934.

Gokak, V. K. "A Brief Note on Indianisms in Indian English." *English in India: Issues and Problems*. Ed. R. S. Gupta and Kapil Kapoor. New Delhi: Academic Foundation, 1991.

Gopalkrishnan, G. S. "Some Observations on the South Indian Pronunciation of English." *Teaching English* 6.2 (1960): 62-67.

Greenbaum, Sidney. "Language Variation and Acceptability." *TESOL Quarterly* 9.2 (1974): 165-72.

Halliday, M. A. K., A. McIntosh, and P. Strevens. *The Linguistic Sciences and Language Teaching*. London: Longman, 1964.

Hockett, Charles F. *A Course in Modern Linguistics*. London : Macmillan, 1958.

Hornby, A. S. *Oxford Advanced Learner's Dictionary*. Oxford : Oxford University Press, 2000.

Hornby, A. S., E. V. Gatenby, and H. Wakefield. *The Advanced Learner's Dictionary of Current English*. Oxford: Oxford University Press, 1968.

Huddlestone, Rodney D. *The Sentence in Written English : A Syntactic Study Based on an Analysis of Scientific Texts*. Cambridge : Cambridge University Press, 1971.

Hudson, Richard. *Word Grammar*. Oxford: Basil Blackwell Ltd., 1986.

Hughes, A., and P. Trudgill. *English Accents and Dialects : An Introduction to Social and Regional Varieties of British English*. London: Arnold, 1979.

Jacobs, Roderick A., and Peter S. Rosenbaum. *English Transformational Grammar*. New Delhi: Wiley Eastern Limited, 1976.

Jensen, E., and T. Vinther. "Exact Repetition as Input Enhanced in Second Language Acquisition." *Language Learning* 53.3 (2003): 373-428.

Jespersen, Otto. *Essentials of English Grammar*. London: George Allen and Unwin Ltd., 1938.

Jones, Charles, and John M. Anderson. *Phonological Structure and the History of English*. New York: North-Holland Publishing Company, 1977.

Jones, Daniel. *The Pronunciation of English*. London: Cambridge University Press, 1958.

Kachru, Braj. B. *Asian Englishes Beyond the Canon*. New Delhi: Oxford University Press, 2005.

——. "Englishization and Contact Linguistics." *World Englishes* 4.2 (1994): 223-32.

——. "Indian English." Special Issue on *Literature and Society*. Seminar MS. 359. 1989. 30-35.

——. "Indian English: A Sociolinguistic Profile of a Transplanted Language." *Studies in Language Learning* 1.2 (1976): 139-89.

——. "Indian English: A Study in Contextualization." *In Memory of J. R. Firth*. London: Longman, 1966.

——. *Indianization of English : The English Language in India*. Delhi: Oxford University Press, 1983.

——. Introduction. In N. K. Aggarwal. *English in South Asia : A Bibliographical Survey of Resources,* Gurgaon and New Delhi: India Documentation Service, 1982: 9-28.

——. "Lexical Innovations in South Asian English." *International Journal of the Sociology of Language* 4 (1975): 55-74.

——. "Models for Non-Native Englishes." *The Other Tongue: English Across Cultures*. New Delhi: Oxford University Press, 1996. 48-74.

——. "South Asian English: Toward an Identity in Diaspora." *South Asian English: Structure, Use, and Users*. Ed. R. J. Baumgardner. Delhi : Oxford University Press, 1996. 9-28.

——. *The Alchemy of English : The Spread, Functions and Models of Non-Native Englishes.* New Delhi: Oxford University Press, 1986.

——. "The Indianness in Indian English." *Word* 21 (1965) : 391-410.

——., ed. *The Other Tongue: English Across Cultures*. Urbana, IL: University of Illinois Press, 1982.

——. "World Englishes and English-Using Communities." *Annual Review of Applied Linguistics* 17 (1997): 66-87.

Kachru, Yamuna. "Culture, Style, and Discourse Expanding Noetics of English." *The Other Tongue: English Across Cultures*. Ed. Braj B. Kachru. Delhi: Oxford University Press, 1996. 340-52.

——. "Discourse Analysis, Non-Native Englishes and Second Language Acquisition Research." *World Englishes* 4.2 (1985) : 223-32.

——."Linguistics and Written Discourse in Particular Languages : Contrastive Studies: English and Hindi." *Annual Review of Applied Linguistics* 3 (1983): 50-77.

Kapur, Manju. *Difficult Daughters*. New Delhi: Penguin, 1998.

Karttunen, L. "Some Observations on Factivity." *Papers in Linguistics* 4.1 (1971): 55-69.

Kirparsky, Paul, and Carol Kiparsky. "Fact." *Semantics: An Interdisciplinary Reader in Philosophy, Linguistics and Psychology*. Ed. Danny D. Steinberg and Leon A. Jakobovits. Cambridge : Cambridge University Press, 1971. 345-69.

Krishnamurthi, Bh. "Spelling Pronunciation in Indian English" *Indian Writing inEnglish*. Ed. Ramesh Mohan. Madras : Orient Longman, 1978. 129-39.

Lyster, R. "Recasts, Repetition, and Ambiguity in L2 Classroom Discourse." SSLA 20 (1998) : 51-81.

Manfred, Gorlach. *Text Types and the History of English*. New York: Mouton de Gruyter, 2004.

Mistry, Rohinton. *A Fine Balance*. Noida: Penguin Books, 2003.

——. *Such A Long Journey*. Noida: Penguin Books, 2002.

Moag, Rodney F. "The Life Cycle of Non-Native Englishes: A Case Study." *The Other Tongue : English Across Cultures*. Ed. Braj B. Kachru. Delhi: Oxford University Press, 1996. 233-54.

Mohan, Ramesh, ed. "Some Aspects of Style and Language in Indian English Fiction." *Indian Writing in English*. Madras: Orient Longman, 1978.

Murata, K. "Intrusive or Co-operative? A Cross-Cultural Study of Interruption." *Journal of Pragmatics* 21 (1994): 385-400.

Murata, K. "Repetitions: A Cross-Cultural Study." *World Englishes* 14.3 (1995) : 343-56.

Nagarajan, S. "Some Historical Notes on the Decline of English." *Journal of Higher Education* 2.3 (1977): 341-49.

——."The Decline of English in India: Some Historical Notes." *College English* 34.7 (1981): 663-70.

Nakajima, Heizo. "Complementizer Selection." *The Linguistic Review* 13.2 (1996): 143-49.

Narasimhaiah, C. D. *The Swan and the Eagle : Essays on Indian English Literature*. 2nd ed. Shimla : Indian Institute of Advanced Study, 1987.

Narayan, R. K. *Swami and Friends*. Mysore : Indian Thought, 1971.

——. *The Bachelor of Arts*. Mysore: Indian Thought, 1965.

——. *The Vendor of Sweets*. Mysore : Indian Thought, 1967.

Pandit, Tukoji R. "Thick Indian Accents." 12 April. 2006. <http://www.samachar.com/features/081203-features.html- 65k>.

Parasher, S. V. "Indian English: Certain Grammatical, Lexical and Stylistic Features." *English World-Wide* 4.1 (1983) : 27-42.

——. *Indian English : Functions and Form*. New Delhi : Bahri Publications, 1991.

Perrin, L., D. Deshaies, and C. Paradis. "Pragmatic Functions of Local Diaphonic in Conversation." *Journal of Pragmatics* 35 (2003): 1843-60.

Pike, Kenneth L. "General Characteristics of Intonation." *Intonation: Selected Readings*. Ed. Dwight Bolinger. Harmondsworth, England: Penguin, 1972. 53-82.

Quirk, Randolph, *et al*. *A Grammar of Contemporary English*. London: Longman, 1972.

Quirk, Randolph, Sidney Greenbaum, Geoffrey Leech, and Jan Svartvik, eds. *A Comprehensive Grammar of the English Language*. London : Longman, 1985.

Radford, Andrew. *English Syntax: An Introduction*. Cambridge: Cambridge University Press, 2004.

Ramchand, Kenneth. *The West Indian Novel and Its Background*. New York: Barnes and Nobel, 1970.

Rao, Raja. *Kanthapura*. New Delhi: Orient Paperbacks, 1996.

Ravichandran, T. "Ingestion, Digestion and Revulsion of Food and Culture in Anita Desai's *Fasting, Feasting*." *Lucknow Journal of Humanities* 1.1(2004): 21-30.

Rieger, C. L. "Repetitions as Self-repair Strategies in English and German Conversations." *Journal of Pragmatics* 35 (2004): 47-69.

Rosenbaum, Peter S. *The Grammar of English Pradicate Complement Constructions*, Cambridge : MIT Press, 1967.

Roy, Arundhati. *The God of Small Things*. New Delhi: Penguin, 2002.

Rubdy, Rani. "A Study of Some Written Varieties of Indian English." Diss. CIEFL, Hyderabad, 1981.

Rushdie, Salman. *Midnight's Children*. London: Vintage, 1995.

Saghal, Anju. "Patterns of Language Use in a Bilingual Setting in India." *English Around the World. Sociolinguistics Perspectives*. Ed. Jenny Cheshire. Cambridge : Cambridge University Press, 1991.

Sanyal, Jyoti. *Indlish—The Book for Every English-Speaking Indian*. New Delhi: Viva Books, 2006.

Sawir, E. C. "Keeping Up with Native Speakers : The Many and Positive Roles of Repetition in the Conversations of EFL learners." *Asian EFL Journal*. 6.4 (2004). < http://www.asian-efl-journal.com/december 04 ES.php>.

Selinker, L. "Interlanguage." *Error Analysis: Perspectives on Second Language Acquisition*. Ed. J. C. Richards. London : Longman, 1974.

Selting, M. "Prosody as an Activity-Type Distinctive Cue in Conversation: The Case of So-Called Astonished Question in Repair Initiation." *Prosody in Conversation*. Ed. E. Couper-Kuhen and M. Selting. Cambridge : Cambridge University Press, 1996. 231-70.

Seth, Vikram. *An Equal Music*. New Delhi: Penguin, 2000.

——. *A Suitable Boy*. New Delhi: Penguin, 2003.

Shaw, Willard D. "Asian Student Attitudes Towards English."

English for Cross-Cultural Communication. Ed. Larry E. Smith. London : Macmillan, 1981. 108-22.

Simpson, J. M. "Regularized Intonation in Conversational Repetition." *Repetition in Discourse. Interdisciplinary Perspectives*. Ed. B. Johnstone. Norwood, New Jersey : Ablex Publishing Corporation, 1994. 1-20.

Smith, Larry E. "Spread of English and Issues of Intelligibility." *The Other Tongue: English Across Cultures*. Ed. Braj B. Kachru. Delhi: Oxford University Press, 1996. 75-90.

Spencer, John. "Notes on the Pronunciation Problem." *Shiksha : The Journal of the Education Department*. 1957. 91-97.

Sridhar, Kamal K. *English in Indian Bilingualism*. Delhi: Manohar Publications, 1989.

——. "Sociolinguistic Theory and Non-Native Varieties of English." *Lingua* 68 (1985): 39-58.

——. "The Pragmatics of South Asian English." *South Asian English : Structure, Use, and Users*. Ed. R. J. Baumgardner. New Delhi : Oxford University Press, 1996. 141-57.

Sridhar, S. N. "Toward a Syntax of South Asian English : Defining the Lectal Range." *South Asian English: Structure, Use, and Users*. Ed. R. J. Baumgardner. New Delhi : Oxford University Press, 1996. 55-69.

Sridhar, Kamal K. and S. N. Sridhar. "Bridging the Paradigm Gap: Second-Language Acquisition Theory and Indigenized Varieties of English." *The Other Tongue : English Across Cultures*. Ed. Braj B. Kachru. New Delhi : Oxford University Press, 1996. 91-107.

Subba Rao, G. *Indian Words in English : A Study in Indo-British Cultural and Linguistic Relations*. London : Oxford University Press, 1954.

Sunwani, V. K. "Rohinton Mistry's *A Fine Balance*: A Critique." *Journal of Indian Writing in English* 25 (1997): 107-12.

Tannen, D. "Repetition in Conversation : Toward a Poetics of Talk." *Language* 63.3 (1987): 574-605.

——. *Talking Voices : Repetition, Dialogue, and Imagery in Conversational Discourse*. New York : Cambridge University Press, 1989.

Taylor, Susan. "Preliminary Study of the Stress System in Indian

English." *Division of English as a Second Language*. Urbana : University of Illinois, 1969.

Thundy, Zacharias. "The Origins of Indian English." *CIEFL Bulletin* 12 (1976): 29-40.

Trudgill, P., ed. *Sociolinguistic Patterns in British English*. London: Arnold, 1978.

Uldall, Elizabeth. "Dimensions of Meaning in Intonation." *Intonation : Selected Readings*. Ed. Dwight Bolinger. Harmondsworth, England : Penguin, 1972. 250-58.

Vallins, G. H. *The Best English*. London: Andre Deutsch, 1971.

Van Der Auwera, Johan. "Relative that — a Centennial Dispute." *Journal of Linguistics* 21 (1985): 149-79.

Verma, S. K. "Code-switching : Hindi-English." *Lingua* 38 (1976): 153-65.

——. "Swadeshi English: Form and Function." *New Englishes*. Ed. John Pride. Rowley, Mass.: Newbury House, 1982. 174-87.

——. "Syntactic Irregularities in Indian English." *Indian Writing in English*. Ed. Ramesh Mohan. Madras : Orient Longman, 1978.

——. "The Systemicness of Indian English." *ITL : Review of Applied Linguistics* 22 (1972): 1-9.

Wells, J. C. *Accents of English*. 3 vols. Cambridge : Cambridge University Press, 1982.

Wilson, H. H. *A Glossary of Judicial and Revenue Terms and of Useful Words Occurring in Official Documents, Relating to the Administration of the Government of British India*. 1885. London : W. H. Allen, 1940.

Yadurajan, K. S. *Current English : A Guide for the User of English in India*. New York : Oxford University Press, 2001.

Yule, Henry, and A. C. Burnell. *Hobson-Jobson : A Glossary of Colloquial Anglo Indian Words and Phrases, and of Kindred Terms, Etymological, Historical, Geographical and Discursive*. 1886. New Delhi: Rupa & Co., 2002.

Index